BOOT CAMP

BOOT
CAMP

BOOT CAMP

The Making of a United States Marine

Antonio M. Salinas

Deeds Publishing | Atlanta

Published by Deeds Publishing in Athens, GA
www.deedspublishing.com

Printed in The United States of America

Cover design and text layout by Mark Babcock

Library of Congress Cataloging-in-Publications data is available upon request.

ISBN 978-1-947309-09-8

Books are available in quantity for promotional or premium use. For information, email info@deedspublishing.com.

First Edition, 2017

10 9 8 7 6 5 4 3 2 1

To my wife Dr. Claire Telford and my children Roman and Shannon. You are my world.

A FIRE FIGHT, JUNE 2009

BOOM!

The Earth, my MRAP, and the air itself shuddered from the explosion of the RPG. That was one sound I will never forget. Time stopped and the battle played before my eyes as if I watched a movie.

A boom of an RPG is the epitome of fear and dread. This boom was not like the fireworks or simulated munitions I had heard before. This sound was Death. I have always wondered what a demon or a dragon from the tales of lore might have sounded like until that moment. Truly, the gates of hell were there in Kunar, and her demons, equipped with Soviet weapons, charged toward us, wanting our souls and our bodies.

The haze of the sun-drenched valley halted all things and life itself. I stared into the highlands, unable to draw a breath. My eyes scanned the rocks, which looked just like the mountains of North Eastern Mexico. The very mountains appeared to glow with heat and hatred for us. They concealed Death. I felt paralyzed in that moment. This was my first action with my platoon. I stared, thinking a thousand thoughts all at once.

Warriors can freeze in these moments because their soul touches the shores of the River Styx. My feet were wet from her waters and I touched the other side. The soul steps one leg out of the body and feels life and death in the same instant.

KA-KA-KA-KA! KA-KA-KA-KA! KA-KA-KA-KA! POP-POP-POP!

My platoon's return gunfire brought my soul back into my body and I could again function in this intricate dance of war. Our trucks replied with horrible songs played by .50 cals, 240's, and my MRAP's MK19.

"Honaker Miracle this is Dagger 46. We are receiving RPG and Small Arms Fire at Grid... We are returning fire at this time." My voice was remarkably clear and I have no idea how in God's name I was able to send up a contact report.

The ground around our vehicles lit up with the impacts of incoming bullets. The dust kicked up and told of the death which was seeking us. We replied with a menu of munitions hurled toward the enemy. Our vehicles continued rocking back and forth so as to prevent the enemy from acquiring a flawless sight picture on us.

Together we took this forbidden dance, the enemy and us. Each of us seeking to rip each other into shreds.

In the midst of the crackle and explosions of battle, I heard something else. I heard my gunner PFC Cortez breathing heavily as he peppered the highlands with 40mm grenades from his MK 19. Hearing him breathe reminded me of what we were. We were animals that wanted many things, but above all—we wanted to live. PFC Cortez's shallow breaths were reminders at how fragile all men truly are in the face of lead projectiles.

"Cortez," I said to him. "Control your rate of fire. You are going to be fine."

"Roger that," Cortez replied.

The world was on fire as my platoon and the enemy traded bullets.

That evening I returned to our combat outpost and reflected on the day's events. It was my first firefight, yet there was something oddly familiar about the sensations I experienced. The intensity, fear, and the chaos of battle reminded me of a place thousands of miles away from the Pech River Valley, Kunar, Afghanistan. The feelings I had that day reminded me of that God forsaken island in South Carolina — Parris Island.

ARRIVAL: PARRIS ISLAND

You never forget your first moments on Parris Island. The sweat, anxiety, and the nerves. This moment is forever imprinted on your mind. For a Marine, it is more memorable than your first love, and maybe even your first battle.

I awoke slowly, as the bus glided through the front gate of the Island. My longboat continued on the stretch of highway that spanned the marshlands separating the island from the mainland. Ignoring my recruiter's advice, I was still wearing my contact lenses and I rubbed away the sleep that clouded my vision. A heavy breath left my lungs as I sighed deeply and stared out the window. A crooked smile graced my face as I watched the moon dance upon the dark waters. I attempted to swallow again, but it was horribly difficult to do so.

The young men around me began to stir. The anxiety in the air, combined with the changing speed of the bus, stirred the recruits awake. I looked into the eyes of the recruit who sat next to me and did not say a single word to him. We merely nodded our heads to one another in the fashion that only warriors know. This head nod is a part of learning to suck it the fuck up. We acknowledged that we were embarking into this hell with one another.

"What the fuck did I get myself into?" I said under my breath.

The span of bridge ended and I continued toward the abyss.

Out of the darkness, the lights of the base slowly crept into view. Buildings materialized out of the darkness and took form. The young men, along with myself, peered out from the window of the vessel and attempted to make sense out of this place. Not a soul on board was asleep now. I was on that place that haunted me and existed only in warrior lore and the prolific movie of my youth: "Full Metal Jacket."

This was real. There was no getting out of it now. I was in for one of the greatest shocks of my lifetime. I was entering a place that would forever change who I was and what defined me as both a man and a warrior.

Welcome to my nightmare.

The speed of the bus continued to slow down as it entered the main side of Parris Island. It was my first time on a military base and it didn't look like what I expected. I saw buildings and the glow of streetlights swarming with insects in the warm and humid summer air. I did not expect that a hell on Earth would appear so normal.

Sweat began to form like dew on a morning field upon my hands. Any man or woman that has become a Marine, or at least attempted it, can recall this moment. Writing about it now reawakens very ancient feelings and emotions I have not felt in years. My hands turn cold as I walk upon this tapestry yet again. My heart rate increased as we approached the recruit receiving area.

Let it begin.

The bus's halt was sounded not by trumpets, but rather the screeching of brakes. In that pause, I wondered what would happen next. I mean, I had seen it in movies and heard about this moment like facing a dragon in nightmarish fairy tales. But, let me tell you something. No movie or words will ever come close to giving this moment justice.

"GET OFF MY BUS!"

The door to the bus opened. Like the first time I heard a bullet whiz overhead in battle, I didn't think it was real, but this was happening. There was a sick utter silence in that tenth of a second between the opening of the door and one of Lucifer's servants stepping onto the bus. I focused on that fatal funnel and waited to see this man who only existed in my nightmares.

He boarded the bus like an Achilles, unmatched in strength by any recruit who sat there before him. Although the lights to the bus illuminated the center aisle, I could not make out his face. I will never forget this man, and sadly I do not know his name. He lives there now and I can still make out his striking silhouette outlined by his tan uniform and distinctive "smoky bear" hat (campaign cover in Marine speak). The Devil might as well have stood in that bus, and he would not have been any more imposing than this Marine who stood in front of me. He was God as far I was concerned. I would follow his words and the words of those like him until my body failed me — and then a few hundred meters more.

SEMPER FI

Some warriors wonder if they will be ready for the chaos known as combat when their time finally comes. Some men just know they are ready.

Modern militaries attempt to condition their young warriors to function properly in the perils of war. The Armed forces use a myriad of tools, ranging from physical training, weapons training, and indoctrination to prepare men and women for the ultimate test of combat. However, there is one common problem that exists in any modern-day training model. One can never fully replicate the chaos of battle in a training environment.

There is one branch of the United States Armed Forces that closely replicates the levels of fear, intensity, and chaos one experiences in battle during its initial training: **The United States Marine Corps.**

Marines are just different. If you are one, or if you ever looked one in the eyes up close, you know they are just different. They possess the ability to stare and rip into your soul with the intensity of a screaming bullet. Marines, walk, talk, and fight differently. What exactly is the reason?

Some may think that it is merely because they run further or lift more weights than the other services. Maybe, their uniforms look cooler. What is it about them that make them so different?

The shock of battle is nearly impossible to put into words or to replicate in anything short of combat itself. However, in my years of training and interlaced with firefights, I realized the Marines have discovered a method to nearly replicate this fearsome and unholy experience. The Marine Corps has found that magic formula to replicate the feeling and intensity of battle. Like, growing bacteria in a culture—the Marines discovered a way to grow and utilize fear in this cell culture of Parris Island and MCRD (Marine Corps Recruit Depot) San Diego. To this day, I am still puzzled and revel at the raw efficiency. War is not a fixed science. Hence making warriors is not a fixed science either. However, it seems the Marines have come as close as one can to making this perfect formula for warriors.

This is one story.

CHOICE

"Hey man! I'm joining the Marines!" I said to Cary.

Cary had a brother serving in the Marines at the time. He looked at me with his cool sarcastic smile and said, "Cool man."

For seventeen-year-old boys, that was all the approval needed for a decision whose repercussions would ripple throughout a lifetime and send me to the dark, savage, and untamed places of the Earth.

Cary walked off to class, leaving me alone for a few moments. It was an early September afternoon during my senior year of high school at one of Detroit's small suburbs, Allen Park. I paused and watched the beautiful sunlight dancing on the tile floor. Somehow, I knew that this peaceful innocence would soon be traded for a world lit aflame.

There's just something about a public high school that is so special and sacred. Somewhere in between the stresses of fitting in, college anxiety, classes, and sporting events lie the critical human elements which give us a special place in the animal kingdom: hope and inspiration.

Cary was gone and I simply enjoyed a few moments by myself, staring into the dark blue paint of my locker. I proudly gazed at the Eagle Globe and Anchor sticker I had recently added to the artwork of my personal collage. This coveted sticker displaying the Marines emblem was a small token; from the recruiter's office I visited the week prior. Although, I had not yet earned the title, the mere idea that I planned to take on such a challenge was enough to incur some bragging rights.

I had a small mirror hanging there and I stared deeply into the depths of my dark eyes. I have always thought that our eyes are such curious things. Our faces and skin wrinkle, but the eyes themselves remain unchanged as they stare back into your soul. I walked into this same darkness each time I stared into a mirror.

Class was starting soon. I looked back at the Eagle Globe and Anchor sticker shining in the sunlight. I daydreamed and wondered what fates awaited me in the summer and years to come. I shut my locker and walked off to class.

SAYING GOOD BYE

I graduated High School in May of 1998. I had the grades to make it into college and I even dreamed of becoming a history teacher. However, there was something inside me that drew me to the song of war. I needed something else.

JULY 12, 1998 – ALLEN PARK, MICHIGAN

I opened my eyes for the last time in my childhood bedroom. It was the last time I rose from a peaceful slumber as a civilian. I looked at the wall and gazed upon my teenage glories as I cleared my head from sleep and allowed my vision to clear. My trophies from various sporting events and belts from Karate came into view. Boys hold onto these glories. For some men, it is all they will ever have. Warriors however, have a different fate. I would leave behind these trinkets. I left the remnants of my civilian self and my very identity behind. It is always hard to get out of bed when you can sense the dark storm waiting for you just outside.

I made my childhood bed, taking my time in the darkness of my basement bedroom. The morning's dim light gently flowed from the room's solitary window. I sighed with a bit of fear and began to question my life's decision. The power of a mere signature can send waves through the fragile stream of destiny. Following a hasty breakfast, I drove to church and attended service at St. Frances Cabrini. Being a young man, I did not have too many sins as of yet, but still, as a guilt driven Catholic, I deemed it necessary to cleanse my soul through confession.

Following church, I made my rounds to some of my friend's houses. I visited my dear boyhood friends and my friend's mother, Ms. Deciccio, invited me over for lunch. It was the last homemade meal that I would have for about three months. I hugged her good bye. As I walked to my car, she gazed upon me as if I was her own son, departing on some God-forsaken conquest. She stood there in her doorway watching me move away, holding on to those final moments like the last bits of sunset on a cold winter day. Perhaps she prepared herself for when her own son would depart for the deserts of Iraq and the mountains of Afghanistan in the years to come.

YOUNG LOVE

Falling in love before going off to war or service is a timeless phenomenon. Young women have been falling hopelessly in love with warriors as they march off to war since Troy. Recruits march off to the military with an enthusiasm that is matched only by gifted musicians, artists and (God help them) writers. They enter the prime of their enthusiastic visions. No heart, be it male or female, is able to withstand this warm glow of charisma.

I met my first love, Lindsay, in the fall of my senior year. First loves always hold a special place in our hearts, and although we marry, have families, and walk all across the earth, we never forget them. The "firsts" always linger there like ghosts in the halls of our memories. Even, if we never see them again, we can recall their faces in a heartbeat.

I arrived and parked at my familiar spot outside of her house, like the countless times during our courtship. She opened the front door and our eyes met. The look upon her face conveyed the story of a thousand heartbreaks. Her beautiful hazel eyes glimmered brilliantly, lubricated by the tears welling up from the very depths of her heart. We attempted to take a walk and talk, but soon decided that her backyard would be more appropriate.

I tried to make her happy, but it was no use, as I could barely hold back my own tears. I held her close as we swung on her swinging chair in her backyard. I ran my fingers through her beautiful auburn hair and allowed her familiar perfume of berberry to flow through my nostrils. I began to question my own destiny. I could not imagine with my own emotions in turmoil how a 17-year-old girl could bear such sadness.

As we spoke, solitary tears fell upon her cheek
Such sadness
I wiped them with my young hand
Trying to erase the sadness

As I held her close to my chest, I felt like I was a father embracing a frightened child. I looked at my watch and realized that dreadful character called "time" had finally caught up to me. I wished that moment together with her would never end. The thing about men is that concepts such as pride and honor can blind us. Sometimes it is not until everything we hold dear is taken away that we realize what we have.

Time tapped me on the shoulder and reminded me of my duty. The two of us slowly walked into the house with dread tucking at my soul. I wished her parents farewell. My eyes shifted to the door and I knew what awaited. We walked together to my truck. It was time.

I kissed her and embraced her tightly. Our eyes met and I watched as the tears slowly rolled from her face like a brook in the forest. Instantly, sadness shoved a lump that weighed ten tons into my throat, and it sank into the depths of my soul. I could no longer hold my tears in and they began to fall like raindrops in a summer storm. I gave her one last kiss good bye, kissing my fingers and placing them upon her lips. To this day, I still remember what she looked like. Her picture in that moment should be placed in the dictionary next to the word "sadness." The white of her eyes were red and surrounded her magical irises.

"I love you and I'll write as soon as I can," my final words to her.

She handed me a card and made a beeline for her house. I watched her gorgeous hair sway back and forth like a wheat field dancing in the wind. With tears distorting my vision, I gazed upon the girl that I loved, knowing I would not see her again for at least 13 weeks.

I continued my drive home. I felt a very strange emotion that seemed to combine utter sadness with glory, an emotion I would later feel prior to my first firefight. I shouted, "Victory!"

I would become a Marine or die trying.

I walked into my house feeling a complete sense of urgency. I gathered up my few allotted necessities and good luck charms. From Cary, I received half of a wishbone from which he said he had won in my favor. Lindsay gave me a charm of a guardian angel that her father had given her, and my younger sister Rachel gave me some lucky fish.

It was time to leave my childhood home behind and begin my training as a United States Marine. Mom, Dad, Rachel, and my cousin Joanna drove me to the recruiting station. My recruiter, SSgt Williams, was there to receive us. The goodbye, in true military fashion was extremely short-lived. I kissed my mother, sister, and cousin good bye. My father and I shook hands and he wished me good luck. My family left me and I sought out the womb of Parris Island to be reborn as a Warrior.

SSgt Williams drove the small group of recruits to the hotel near MEPs (Military Enlisting Processing center) in Warren, Michigan. Of those accompanying me was a boy named John Smiles. I went to high school with John and he helped talk me into joining the Marines. However, he would not pass the trials himself.

I arrived at the hotel and had dinner with the voucher the Marines provided me. I called my mother, whose voice was choked up by tears. Linda's was the same.

Following dinner, I joined a few other enlistees and went out on the town. We tried to make the best of our final hours of freedom. We went to the nearby bowling alley. We made small talk with the locals until about 3:00 am and arrived back at the hotel around 3:30 am. I had to be downstairs at 4:15am. I slept my final peaceful moments. I truly could not foresee what I was about to experience. There are times in one's life where a mere 15-minute nap can feel as refreshing as a seven-hour sleep.

I shared my breakfast in the company of other young men who shared the beachhead of destiny with me. A group of 20 of us from different services met up and departed for MEPS. In classic military style, the majority of the morning was filled with "hurry up and wait." Following lunch, we were ushered into the enlisting room. An officer stood in front of us and ushered the oath that I have both sworn to and given to men under my command later in my career:

I, state your name, do solemnly swear to support and defend the constitution of the United States, against all enemies, foreign and domestic, that I will bear true faith and allegiance to the same. And that I will obey the orders of the President of the United States and the orders of the officers appointed over me. According to the regulation and the Uniform code of Military justice. So help me God.

THAT NIGHT

My voyage to Boot camp was an unforgettable experience. It will stay with me for my entire life. I attempted to cherish my final moments of peace before I shed my clothes and began my time in that god-forsaken womb known as Parris Island.

I awoke from my sleepless night at the hotel near MEPS. The Sgt on duty handed the packets and meal vouchers to John Smiles. The Sgt wished us good luck and we departed for Detroit Metropolitan airport.

I wore a bright red Nautica shirt and khakis, conservative attire as directed by the Marine Corp's pamphlet. Once dropped off at the airport, there was no denying that I would soon enter a new world. My final meal consumed as a civilian in Detroit was at Pizza Hut.

It is always terribly difficult to eat when you are afraid. You don't fully digest the sustenance and your stomach does not accept it. I think this is a survival complex from times of when we were hunted by wild beasts. It was the same for me before football games and later in actual combat. Eating is always easier after the battle has been fought.

I munched and munched with a few of my fellow recruits. I tried to bullshit with my mates, but the mood was difficult to keep light. The storm that awaited in South Carolina continued to stir up within my stomach, soul, and mind. I was moving toward a new life and the Marines. I was about to start my journey in that horrible hell known as Parris Island. It would not be long now.

The unhappy feast was soon concluded. I threw out the last pizza box that I would have in months. It's a strange feeling when you are about to leave ᵃ ᶜⁱᵛⁱˡⁱzation. I began to cherish even the subtlest of comforts. I stared at the grease laden cardboard pizza box in the trash. Writers always have their heads in the clouds; especially before they realize they are writers. Throwing away that pizza box was like a piece of my civilian self being discarded. Like a serpent shedding his skin, my transformation was beginning.

This scene would, in fact, be one of the last moments that I would blend in as a part of the civilian herd. I boarded my flight, surrounded by a sea of civilians. For the time being, I was one of those sheep who over obsessed with material items such as cars, houses, and money. I chose a different way of life, but we had not yet crossed the river. My coat remained white, fluffy, and soft.

I could not sleep on the flight. I did not have a direct flight and headed toward my layover in Dallas. My small group deplaned and headed into the terminal. I began moving to my next gate, which was set to depart within the hour. During the walk, I instantly sensed the other small groups of sheep who prepared for their shearing at Parris Island. Small groups of cocky and fit young men were walking toward the same destination.

Along my route, a Marine Corporal crossed my path. His tan uniform looked as if it was painted on his muscles. I stopped as he approached, standing there like a shy pony captivated by a stallion; hoping that I too would look like him one day, galloping upon the fields of war.

He asked, "Where you guys going?"

"Parris Island." A few of the recruits answered with reverberating pride.

"Awesome, guys! Don't worry. You'll love it."

He continued his walk and faded away into the airport and into the annals of my memory.

The Marine's words echoed in my head as we neared the gate. Would I love it? For that matter, would I graduate from boot camp? My trial of a lifetime was soon approaching and my mind drifted to so many things.

I finally arrived at the gate of departure that would take me to my final destination: "Charleston, South Carolina." Several dozen young men in the flower of their youth began to congregate in line. Already I felt the tension in the air. Humans, after all, are beasts of the field, and emit certain emotions when stressed. All warriors know this tension. It is that certain type of fear in those moments prior to departure. I came to know it again, in those final moments prior to battle in Afghanistan.

Becoming accustomed to this tension is the difference and advantage that professional Warriors have over the edge of insurgents. Warriors become almost desensitized over time to such stresses, through training.

FLIGHT

Flights in the modern military age become longboats for those transcending that strange voyage between the land of the living and the dead. Walking on the tramway, I was in a controlled air-conditioned platform, comfortable, and well fed. I still walked amongst the civilian population, the very sheep responsible for running this civilization. They graze and work under the shadow of a warrior's shield. Soon it would be my duty to protect them.

I ushered to my seat, buckled in, and awaited that god-awful mind numbing safety brief given by the stewardesses.

"Nice weather in Charleston this evening. The temperature is about 85 degrees and clear skies. Flight time is going to be at two hours and thirty minutes. Sit back and enjoy my flight," the pilot said.

"Enjoy my flight," I thought.

I almost laughed as I stared at the cooling vent above my head. "Fuck." I thought, as this adventure and fantasy was fast becoming my reality. It was easy to point out those with me who were going to the Island. I saw it in their prepared bodies. But, most of all I saw it in their faces; that unmistakable look of dread. All warriors know this look. I saw this look in the eyes men who knew they were going on a particularly difficult mission, years after this experience.

So how does one truly deal with embarking in a life changing experience that will forever shred who they are? Within hours I would embark on a journey that would transform my life, personality, identity, and very well the fate of my unborn descendents. This choice ensured that I would taste that peculiar forbidden wine known as battle. Luckily, warriors around the world have learned a way to cope with such pressures. Do you think we stay awake and contemplate the horrible fates that are sure to await us? The answer is no. Rather, like many, I chose to ignore that pesky thing known as fear. Instead I slept.

I fell into one of the most satisfying sleeps in my life. Perhaps, it was because for the brief moment in time I was free from the storm that I would soon join. I closed my eyes and dreamed of sweet nothings. I dreamed of home, my bedroom, and of fond summers "up north" in Michigan. It was a lovely rest.

The decent of the plane stirred me awake. I rubbed the sleep from my eyes and saw that many of the men around me were doing the same. I was beginning my awakening toward a new life and to a new world. The thing about the military is that I thought I had an idea of exactly what I was getting myself into. I soon found out that I was dead wrong.

My plane landed in Charleston and I waited anxiously to get up and out of my seat. This was it. Something about waiting to debark off a plane always drives many of us crazy. This happens regardless of whatever type of trip you may be embarking on. On the cusp of a life-changing event such as Marine Corps Boot Camp, this normally inconvenient wait became excruciatingly even more horrible.

I watched as the dozens of overweight businessmen slowly lifted themselves out of their plush first class seats in expensive poorly fitting suits. They carried their briefcases and other notes for what I was sure were important meeting in their boring consumer lives. At that moment, I realized, I was judging them. Perhaps I was jealous of their comfortable lives and their big figure salaries.

I wonder if the sheep dog ever despises those sheep that he selflessly protects from the evil of the world. Does he ever realize that the farmer cares more for these fat defenseless poofs of wool that exist only to graze, fuck, and make money for the farmer. It was one of the first times in my life where I realized that I was judging the herd in such a manner. They continued their slow pathetic strolls out of the plane.

To my flanks, the stirring of the other recruits near me was unmistakable. A blind man could have seen and sensed the increased anxiety of the herd. Soon, the row to my front was empty. Time had again shown her dreaded face. There was no getting out of it now.

I grabbed the only items that I was permitted to bring on this epic sojourn for America's warriors. I had a hygiene bag packed with deodorant, shaving cream, a few razors, toothbrush, toothpaste, and an address book, as cell phones were not widely proliferated as of yet.

I began the slow walk in the center of the aircraft toward the door. The young stewardess's beauty struck me as she said her farewell to us. I could tell that she knew who we were and where we were going. Her hazel eyes glimmered beautifully in the lights of the galley way. Her wonderful curls danced upon her shoulders and down toward her curves. All the men looked at her the same way that I did. I knew I had to savor one last sip of beauty before we engaged on this path. Our eyes met and she said such beautiful fitting words.

"Thanks for flying Delta."

Being a warrior for many years reminded me that humans are in fact animals. The sensations of fear, anger, and anxiety can be smelled, tasted, and felt. All one must do is listen to the earth and those beings around you. I assure you will feel and know them.

I walked on the tramway, taking in the final moments of peace before entering the storm. It is these final moments where I savored the subtle nuances of comfort and peace. I remembered how the soft ground felt as I walked in my comfortable running shoes. The light from the terminal glowed at the end of the sky bridge. I was nearing hell's gates.

That was when I first saw them; Marines. A few Marine Non-commissioned officers stood there, lying in wait for us. The group was composed of Corporals and Sergeants. They did not yell at that moment; there was no need. The magic of Parris Island was already compelling me to follow orders without hesitation.

The Marines calmly instructed my group to be quiet and ushered the words that echo through the heads of all combat leaders: "Follow me." I followed these wolves and did not utter a word to my mates. I walked like I would on hundreds of combat patrols later in life. I walked with the uncertainty of the unknown. I was strong, fit, and confident. These were my only tools for survival here, and they would have to carry me through this storm.

Following this few hundred-meter walk, I entered one of those small side doors present in all airport terminals. I continued making turns in this labyrinth whose walls were composed of those cylindered blocks covered with yellow paint. The Marines led us into a large conference room and ordered us to sit. There were maybe 50 of us in this small room.

The Sergeant in charge introduced himself and in classic Marine Corps fashion, he provided the timeline of events for the rest of the evening. I listened as the hour was fast approaching midnight.

"You're not at Parris Island, yet. So you can relax; just keep it down."

I ate my final meal in peace and without my feet at the position of attention. They provided us with a sandwich, chips, and a soda. It was a meal that we were later taught to call "bag-nasties." The other recruits and I attempted to make small talk with one another. In years to come, things such as bullshitting calmly to another comrade could calm one's nerves better than a double of Maker's Mark on the rocks.

For the first and only time in my life, I had blonde highlights in my hair. I chuckled with one of the other recruits as it blatantly obvious that they were not natural. In turn he asked me, "Do you think I can request a personal day once we arrive at the Island?"

We both laughed at the absurdity of the question.

The Marines played a video that went over the requirements of becoming a Marine. I would have to pass written exams, a physical fitness test, the swim test, qualify with a rifle, and survive the Crucible. There were more requirements that were not presented in the video, but these were the main ones.

"Alright, on your feet and make sure you have everything that you brought with you in your hands."

I again entered this yellow painted corridor, walking like death herself, quietly and with a purpose. The time was well after midnight now. I listened to my nervous footsteps quietly echo off the cold tile. The neon lights showered uncomforting light upon my tired eyes. I smelled the nervous cold sweat permeating through my shirt and from the other recruits near me. The beast called Parris Island was close now.

I exited a door where a few buses were staged. They were to be my boat to the other side and to the world of darkness, pain, power, and glory. I did not have to provide any offering to this boatman; as I had already paid my toll. With a signature from my young hand, I offered almost a half-decade of service to my lords. The clear majority of recruits offered four years of active service with another four in individual ready reserve service.

The Marines placed us in ragtag formations and filed us aboard these dark vessels with cushioned seats and rubber tires. I found my seat and attempted to swallow my fears away, but it didn't work.

"It's about an hour drive to the Island. I suggest you get some sleep, because it's the last you are going to get for a while," a corporal said to us.

I wondered how in God's name I was supposed to sleep at a time like this. The buses departed one after another and started their voyage toward Parris Island. My voyage continued upon these dark highways shrouded by the South Carolina night air.

Sleep came to me. I think Mars cannot bear to watch his warriors squirm needlessly in the womb over such things as anticipation. I fell into a wonderful sleep and dreamed of nothing. I would become reborn into a world whose lessons are lectured by the whizzes and cracks of incoming bullets.

ARRIVAL: PARRIS ISLAND

I awoke slowly, as the bus glided through the front gate of the Island. My longboat continued on the stretch of highway that spanned the marshlands separating the island from the mainland. Ignoring to my recruiter's advice, I was still wearing my contact lenses and I rubbed away the sleep that clouded my vision. A heavy breath left my lungs as I sighed deeply and stared out the window. A crooked smile graced my face as I watched the moon dance upon the dark waters. I attempted to swallow again, but it was horribly difficult to do so.

The young men around me began to stir. The anxiety in the air, combined with the changing speed of the bus, stirred the recruits awake. I looked into the eyes of the recruit who sat next to me and did not say a single word to him. We merely nodded our heads to one another in the fashion that only warriors know. This head nod is a part of learning to suck it the fuck up. We acknowledged that we were embarking into this hell with one another.

"What the fuck did I get myself into?" I said under my breath.

The span of bridge ended and I continued toward the abyss. Out of the darkness, the lights of the base slowly crept into view. Buildings materialized out of the darkness and took form. The young men, along with myself, peered out from the window of the vessel and attempted to make sense out of this place. Not a soul on board was asleep now. I was on that place that haunted me and existed only in warrior lore and the prolific movie of my youth: "Full Metal Jacket."

This was real. There was no getting out of it now. I was in for one of the greatest shocks of my lifetime. I was entering a place that would forever change who I was and what defined me as both a man and a warrior.

Welcome to my nightmare.

The speed of the bus continued to slow down as it entered the main side of Parris Island. It was my first time on a military base and it didn't look like what I expected. I saw buildings and the glow of streetlights swarming with insects in the warm and humid summer air. I did not expect that a hell on Earth would appear so normal.

Sweat began to form like dew on a morning field upon my hands. Any man or woman that has become a Marine, or at least attempted it, can recall this moment. Writing about it now reawakens very ancient feelings and emotions I have not felt in years. My hands turn cold as I walk upon this tapestry yet again. My heart rate increased as we approached the recruit receiving area.

Let it begin.

The bus's halt was sounded not by trumpets, but rather the screeching of brakes. In that pause, I wondered what would happen next. I mean, I had seen it in movies and heard about this moment like facing a dragon in nightmarish fairy tales. But, let me tell you something. No movie or words will ever come close to giving this moment justice.

"GET OFF MY BUS!"

The door to the bus opened. Like the first time I heard a bullet whiz overhead in battle, I didn't think it was real, but this was happening. There was a sick utter silence in that tenth of a second between the opening of the door and one of Lucifer's servants stepping onto the bus. I focused on that fatal funnel and waited to see this man who only existed in my nightmares.

He boarded the bus like an Achilles, unmatched in strength by any recruit who sat there before him. Although the lights to the bus illuminated the center aisle, I could not make out his face. I will never forget this man, and sadly I do not know his name. He lives there now and I can still make out his striking silhouette outlined by his tan uniform and distinctive "smoky bear" hat (campaign cover in Marine speak). The Devil might as well have stood in that bus, and he would not have been any more imposing than this Marine who stood in front of me. He was God as far I was concerned. I would follow his words and the words of those like him until my body failed me — and then a few hundred meters more.

The Marine Drill Instructor is the creator of violence, death, attention to detail, and precision. He stood there like a Picasso who painted the world of war with Marines as his different colors. In some respects, I met my new mother that night. He stared through me and my fellow recruits. This moment on the bus lasted no longer than forty-five seconds. However, it rings in my head still like the bullets from my first firefight. In these forty-five seconds or so I learned what fear was.

Violence and pain are a warrior's greatest inspiration. I remember being stung in the face by the Marines. Violence became my mother's milk and I suckled from this bitch wolf like Romulus and Remus did.

Entire chapters can be written on this moment alone, and perhaps it should be. If you are a Marine, have ever met one, or fought along one of them in the heat of battle, you know that one of their reactions to a battle or a problem is ferocity lined with exuding confidence and fearlessness. I learned to become the very thing that made me so horribly nervous. I became fear, shock, and the blood wrenching violence. I learned to become anger and the angel of Death.

He states the words that we can more intimately recall than the "Our Father."

"The first and last things out of your mouth from here on out will be Sir! Do you understand that?"

"Sir, Yes Sir!"

"What?"

"Sir, Yes Sir!"

"At this time, collect everything that you brought with you and get off my Bus!"

"Sir, yes Sir!"

"Move! Move! Move!"

This moment forever lives within my mind and my heart. It has been nineteen years since I charged off that bus and I can recall it more vibrantly than my wedding day.

A human wave of power engendered by the ranks of powerful young Marine recruits resonated in the surrounding atmosphere. There was yelling I remember. But this was a different sort of yelling. Much different than those I might have echoed during high school sporting events or during my martial art exercises.

This type of yelling was so different and puzzled me as I stood out of my seat. It is only after seeing battle do I now know why. The recruits were genuinely frightened. However, warriors learn a distinct reaction when encountering fear. Warriors do not cower like children, or lesser men. Instead they answer fear with an equally more powerful and natural reaction. Warriors answer it with a visceral and primordial anger. Adrenaline laced blood pumps freely through their muscles, turning skin bright red and elevating heart rates. True warriors do not cower nor run like gazelles or rabbits. Rather, they lunge forward into the dark recesses of their greatest fears.

This primordial shock is one of the tenets of the Marine Corps tactical and cultural ethos. It is a culture that attempts to instill fearlessness, strength, and honor into not only its ranks; but into their leadership as well. This wave of violence accompanied us on nearly every single aspect of life on Parris Island. I learned to become violence. I learned to become that Grim Reaper and prepared myself to slaughter the enemy upon the field of battle.

I felt the energy in the air from recruits to both my front and rear. We were charging and shoving one another off the bus as if we were hoplites in the Spartan Phalanxes in the pass of Thermopylae. This entire movement may have lapsed perhaps only 20 seconds of time, but it stings my memory like a car accident that lasted for an entire day.

A few tenths of a second passed and I stood in the door of the bus, attempting to take in my surroundings as only a beast of the field can. The dark night came alive painted by those dim brown lights, the landscape to my front and displayed to me the MCRD recruit receiving building. As I prepared to take my last step off the bus, the objects of Marine Corps lore and training came into my field of view. I saw them: The Yellow Footprints.

YELLOW FOOT PRINTS

The scene unfolded before my eyes like a bad dream. I was very much in the moment, yet at the same time, I was not. There are certain times in my life when it feels as if my soul detaches from my body, and I watch myself move like a Lion in the high grass toward his prey.

There they were; these Yellow Footprints that have been glorified, as if they were the gateway to the Ark of the Covenant in the dozen training videos that I had watched previously. As I hit the pavement, the Drill Instructor broke my small dream sequence by screaming at the top of his lungs and gesturing with his powerful arm toward these yellow guardians of the country.

The Yellow Footprints were amassed in a formation, as I would soon become one. They stood there blessed by the gods of war on land, sea, and air. They called to us with promises of strength, confidence, and glory. These footprints did not welcome the weak, or those void of passion.

I moved onto them and stood there in that neat formation amassed for those who dared to become Marines. The recruits moved to the position of attention with heels locked together and hands hanging loosely at the side. This would be my first and most sloppy position of attention. I was not drilled to flex my muscles, keep my shoulders back, or to keep my thumbs along the seam of my trousers, all lessons that would be drilled into me under the hot southern sun or under the thunderous echoes of my platoon's voices in my barracks.

I stood there staring straight into the head of the recruit to my front. I looked deeply into his beautifully well-groomed head of blonde hair. I was thinking that his hair, as well as mine, would soon be shed onto the ground without regard. However, for the time being; I kept my mane for a bit longer.

The formation of recruits was surrounded by these majestic looking beasts called Drill Instructors. A few of them caroused the ranks looking for any weakness or any wandering eyes. The recruit to my left attempted a quick visual survey of his surroundings. It was a mistake, but his mistake became an unforgettable lesson for all of us.

"What are you looking at recruit? The Drill Instructor asked.

"I wasn't looking."

"I?! Did you just say I?! There is no such thing as I! Do you understand that?!"

The recruit was silenced. I was only standing on Parris Island for a few seconds when I witnessed the pure genius of the Marine Corps training method. To the untrained eye, it may have looked like the Drill Instructor had a legitimate hatred for this recruit, as he shouted with the volume of a thousand gunshots in my ears. At that moment, I truly did know what to think.

The Drill Instructor did not hate this recruit. Rather, he hated failure and defeat. He would not permit us to lose. He would not permit us to disgrace the tenets of the Marine Corps. He was preparing us to not only follow orders under the horror of chaos in battle. Without knowing it, he was already instilling in us the proper tools we would later need to excel in chaos. This screaming and violence would allow me one day to take aim upon the enemy or coolly call in a fire mission while having one foot in the river Styx.

Of course, in that moment I was not thinking with a Clausewitzian mind, thinking of how yelling at a recruit would one day permit him to do his job in battle. In that moment, I was attempting to keep the fear suppressed and shield myself from these angry beasts whose muscular bodies were adorned with brilliant tan and creased shirts, topped off with their campaign covers or in laymen terms, their "smoky bear hats."

"On behalf of the Commanding General, I welcome you to Parris Island. You are now subject to the Uniform Code of Military justice. You will address any civilian, Sailor, or Marine on this installation as Sir! Is that clear???"

"Sir yes Sir!"

"'I can't hear you!"

Sir, yes sir!"

The Drill Instructors continued making corrections on the sloppy half assed formation standing upon these yellow footprints. Recruits and Drill Instructors shouted in reply to these ferocious and unforgiving corrections. Their voices pierced the darkness like lions roaring in the dark African Savannah. It was in this chaos that I strangely felt at home. It felt lovely to be apart of this devastating ritual deeply knitted into the Western Military Tradition.

No storm lasts forever and the yelling suddenly halted.

"Fuck… what's next?" I thought to myself.

One of the greatest sources of fear in Parris Island was the fact that the unknown loomed around every moment. My will or opinion did not matter. All my happiness or pain came from the hands of my masters, the Drill Instructors. They were the lords and keepers of the beloved Eagle Globe and Anchor.

"Listen up! Eyes on me! You are going to file into this building. You will file in, without saying anything, keeping your head and eyes to the front and sit down. Do you understand that?"

"Sir, yes sir!"

Even a simple task like walking into a building was a feat of stress, anxiety, and judgment while on Parris Island. My time on those legendary footprints was coming to an end. I kept my eyes locked on to that head of soft blonde hair, as the files to the right of me began their silent march into the recruit receiving building. There was not a single word ushered.

An eerie and dreadful silence cloaked the movement. The recruits moved into the building as if they were conducting a raid. Soon, it was my turn to walk into the building. The blonde hair in front of started moving and I did not dare avert my eyes. I performed a right turn and the door to building sang it's warning; as if we were entering *Dante's inferno* (abandon all hope, all ye who enter here. What it really said: *Through these portals pass prospects for America's finest fighting force...United States Marines.*

The doors to the processing building were made of steel and shone brilliantly in the darkness. Dual seals of the Eagle, Globe, and Anchor faced out. Defiantly, saying that you would never be good enough to have this title.

Turn around and surrender.

You will never be good enough.

The in-processing building of Parris Island.

The doors.

MARKER, PLATOON 1084

I entered this building whose red floors, cleanliness, and scent instantly triggered my senses. The scent was one of new uniforms, adorned by the swarm of new recruits who inhabited the temporary squad bays, before moving on to their training battalions.

A Drill Instructor greeted us as we walked in and guided us either left or right. It was this moment where my destiny was shaped. Depending on what direction I went decided on which platoon I became a member of. My fate decided, I walked left.

There were about two hundred of us that night. We sat down in the neat, ancient seeming rows of plain desks in the main atrium of the receiving barracks. I was in complete shock and pure disorientation set in.

"Eyes front! Heels together! You're not looking around! You're not touching your face." The Drill Instructors repeated several times.

I did as ordered. In such moments, I began to wonder what in God's name I had gotten myself into. I did my best to do as I was told and kept my eyes locked to the front of the room. Through my peripheral vision, though, I was able to sneak a peek at the ongoing chaos. Dozens of more recruits continued to flood the room wearing their preppy selected clothes. The DIs were herding us like the undisciplined sheep we were.

"Eyes front! If you are on this side of the room you are in Platoon 1084. If you are on this side, you are in Platoon 1085. Now, write this number on the back of your left hand."

Like the majority of things in Recruit training, my fate was decided for me. I was a member of Platoon 1084, C Company, 1st Recruit Training Battalion. With a black marker, I wrote the numbers 1084 on my left palm.

IT BEGINS

The numbers were stained upon my hand and bled into my warrior soul. The magnitude of this moment did not strike me at first. I had only the faintest idea of what in God's name a platoon even was. I mean for fuck's sake walking into this building was stressful enough by itself.

The training began. It was truly an epic sight to see such a group of normally prideful males in the prime of their youth be castrated by fear. Such was the effect of the island. The magic had begun, even before the first drop of sweat hit the sandy earth. We were being molded to become warriors designed to conduct horrible acts of violence on the bodies of our enemies.

A series of different slides was displayed upon a large projection screen. The DIs began their work. The class pertained to the Uniform Code of Military Justice and the proper conduct of a Marine in the fleet. One of the most memorable slides in the class was the following words: ZERO TOLERANCE.

"What does that say recruits?"

"Zero tolerance, sir! That's right! The Marines have Zero Tolerance for illegal substance abuse."

It was no joke. They wanted to make themselves perfectly clear. In coming years, Marines that were found guilty of taking dope were put out of the service without regard or pity.

Next came a flood of paperwork, processing us formally onto Parris Island. The forms came to us non-stop. I began filling them out with personal information. I began inserting myself into this beast called the United States Marines Corps. One of the forms was a postcard with the following information:

"Dear_____

I have safely arrived at MCRD, Parris Island, SC. I will soon begin my training. I will write as soon as I can.

My address is:
REC:_____
PLT_____, ___ CO. ____RTB
MCRD, PARRIS ISLAND, SC 29902

I filled out the information, thinking of my mother's tears as she said her final farewell to me. I wondered what her face would look like when she read this. It was my final farewell as a boy before I entered this abyss. With my information complete, I passed my card to the recruit in front of me.

The DIs made us prepare for the contraband search. I was not dumb enough to attempt to bring anything incriminating with me. The Drill Instructors found a few porno magazines and cigarettes. Nothing major.

The time passed painfully slowly throughout the night. You could sense the sadness of the building. I entered training thinking it will instantly be like the legendary Spartan agoge, controlled by chaos and pain.

In ancient Sparta, history tells us that each child was inspected shortly following birth. Spartan elders inspected each babe for any potential defects that would prevent him from defending his polis against any enemy.

However, in the modern age, the Marines needed to insure that you would not die in the training. This meant around 72 hours of in processing was necessary for us to be measured and to ensure we could at least safely begin training.

SHEDDING SELF

Platoon 1084 was on the island for perhaps three hours now. Yet, in these three hours I can tell you that I was more profoundly affected than the past three years of high school. I honestly was amazed that such a place still existed in the modern age.

Growing up in the superpower of the United States in the late 20th century was a time of supreme arrogance. The last major conflict at the time was fought in 1991 and US forces demolished the Iraqi army in a 100-hour ground war. It seemed that we had regained the honor lost by fighting guerillas in the jungles of Vietnam.

One would think that victory can be achieved via push button technology or with smart bombs. The Marine Corps never forgot the need for effective ground forces. They knew and still know to this day that it takes brave warriors to hold the fragile line of freedom. They knew that regardless of how many billions of dollars we spent on the defense budget a year, that it would still take young men to wear armor and carry rifles to achieve victory. The year was 1998.

One of the beautiful facts regarding the Marine Corps Recruit training model is that it has, for the most part, remained unchanged. Although the fatigue uniforms that the Marines and recruits of Parris Island have changed more than a few times, the fiery intensity of the Drill Instructor and recruits on this God-Forsaken Island remains constant. One of the main goals of the Marine Corps recruit training is not to pass on technical expertise. Rather, it is to properly indoctrinate Marines into a world ruled by chaos.

"On your feet!"

"Sir, yes Sir!" the platoon answered.

Already I was learning to obey. The hour was growing late and the world began to swirl around me. For many recruits, including me, this goes down as one of the worst days of my life. A day ruled by uncertainty, yelling, and a never-ending supply of chaos and anger.

1084 marched outside and was placed into files. I have always marveled at the fascination that western military has with lines. Recruits learned to live, obey, and conquer in such ways. I was beginning to become this phalanx of power and mayhem. 1084 was being herded to have its heads shaved.

Like dozens of sheep being made ready for the shearing, the masters marched the platoon. I stood in my line "nut to butt." The recruits were forced to stay close to one another, much closer than we were used to. Simple civilian norms and discomforts would soon become things of the past for my mates and me. 1084 was being prepared for the fires of hellacious combat. Comfort would soon become one of my least concerns.

"Keep your mouths shut! Keep your eyeballs on that recruit in front of you!"

At the time, I, too, was one of these sheep. I desperately wanted to look around and take in my surroundings. I began to learn this iron discipline that was needed by all Marines. I listened and followed orders. The Marine Corps method of teaching is one of the most effective and devastating mechanisms of instruction to ever grace the world. Even after becoming an Officer and attending Graduate school, I am still in awe of this machine.

Slowly I approached the barbershop. I moved one step at a time, like the sloppy sheep that I still was. I looked and saw what I would soon look like. There were recruits with their heads freshly shaved filtering out of the barbershop and returning to the formation. They began looking the part. It was coming but not completely yet; as the recruits were still all wearing civilian clothes.

A few more feet separated me from looking more like a Marine. I took a moment and inhaled a deep breath. The warm and humid South Carolina air filled my lungs. It was still very much unclear as to what the hell I was doing. Then it was my turn.

A Drill Instructor was in there with the barbers, directing the recruits to chairs. I stared at the men shaving us bald. They were all middle aged, and continued in their emotionless work. I wondered what would compel a barber to conduct this kind of work, especially on this god-forsaken island at this horrible God less hour of the night. These barbers reminded me of those men who worked in slaughterhouses, slaughtering animals without regard. Their faces were void of any emotion.

My turn came up. The Drill Instructor forcefully looked me into the eye and ordered me to sit down. I sat down in the barber's chair and instantly I was bald as is told in Marine Corps legendary cadence.

It was the most unemotional haircut of m life. I felt like an animal being sheared prior to my slaughter. The barber forcefully ran the razor over my freshly highlighted hair. I was staring down and watched as my blonde highlights fell upon the ground. I closed my eyes to attempt to find at least a small piece of peace in the chaos.

With each felled lock of hair was gone more of my identity of a civilian. My just shy of two decades of life was stripped from me and cast down onto a tile floor covered with hair. There would be no need for my hair where I was going. The haircut gives the Marine Corps the uniformity it desires and takes away the life we all left behind. The transformation was moving with incredible speed.

The barber was soon finished with me and took the cape off. I walked toward the hatch of the Shop where a sturdily built recruit was standing. He had been tasked by the Drill Instructor to wipe the excess fur off our disgusting hides. I bent down in front of him and he wiped the hair off my head. I stood up and walked outside, toward my nameless comrades.

DON'T TOUCH YOUR FACE

The sun had not yet graced the South Carolina sky and I was moving non-stop for hours, continuing in-processing into this new and foreign world ruled by the tenets of survival, force, and violence.

"Listen up recruits! When you sit, your backs are straight, shoulders back, eyes to the front, and your hands have your fingers together on your lap. You are not touching your face or looking around."

"Seriously?" I thought.

"Why the fuck can't I touch my face?"

This small lesson is crucial for those attempting to attain a precise shot as a sniper or while lying in wait in an ambush. These small details help attain victory and hold the advantage over the enemy. Honestly look at a Marine. He very rarely touches his face. It is the mark of discipline and of hardened warrior.

They, of course, did not share this tidbit of information with us. Instead, the Drill Instructors utilized the most perfect and easily renewable resource available to them on the island: FEAR. They stated that the constant touching of our faces could cause a disease known as cellulitis, in which inflammation would incur on your face and skin.

It seemed that any number of horrible conditions could be

born upon this piece of swamp with patches of dry land on it. It was best to listen.

FIRST SUNRISE

An in-processing Drill Instructor, SSgt Gomez, was attached to my platoon. A trim muscular man, whose accent gave away his place of origin without a doubt as Puerto Rico. This temporary Drill Instructor was as Virgil was to Dante in the exploration of hell. My Virgil adorned with the campaign cover. He was my shepherd for the next 24 hours or so. He took care of the platoon and taught a few skills necessary for survival on the island.

"When I say EYEBALLS, you say snap Sir and look at me. Got it?"

"Sir, yes sir!"

"When I say EARS, you say open!"

"Yes Sir!"

"The three most important things that you will say to me are Yes Sir! No Sir! And Aye, Aye Sir! (I understand and will comply)."

"If you wish to use the Head (bathroom)."

"Sir, Recruit _____ Requests permission to make a head call."

Only five hours or so into the training and every thing that made me American was suspended: my individual freedom and rights. Americans are lovers of freedom and of individuality. They love their own opinions, the right to vote or not, and their assault rifles.

Here on the island, personal sentiments or feeling were the

least prized objects of all. What mattered was the mission and the pride of the Marine Corps.

What next? I thought; as we were led outside the receiving building. SSgt Gomez assembled us into a ragtag formation, attempting to dress the lines. I stood there, still in a bit of shock from ensuing chaos that the island seemed to emit from its soil. Dawn was approaching and illuminated the recruits and buildings around me in that blue eerie stillness that all warriors are intimately familiar with.

In the military, we call this time of day BMNT or begin morning nautical twilight. The French call this time of day *L'heure bleue*. Artists or photographers call this time of day as the blue hour. This is the time before the sun crosses the horizon. For warriors, it is a very sacred time, whether we are deployed in combat or at home in garrison tucked safely away behind the gates.

This time usually precedes military assaults or operations. It can be a very nerve racking time, knowing that one's platoon was no longer hidden by the night and was now visible to the Taliban. This blue twilight is only reserved for those who are warriors. They accompany marathon runners on their early morning runs or a hunter on opening day of a season. The senses come alive here, and one's eyes seek out prey, be it the open road, a deer, or an armed man. This is the magic hour for warriors.

I was born again on this new sunrise. I had not seen twilight since my last hunt in the fall of that year. Although, I still had my civilian clothes upon my back, I was different. The recruits stood there in the ordered lines standing shoulder to shoulder in a foreign and distant land. Like all writers, I have always been a dreamer, and my mind drifted in the pure military romance of this moment. I thought how wonderful it was to be partaking in this ancient dance of breaking in a new military force.

The western military tradition is one that depends upon the strength of its warriors to conduct their duty in their place in formation. I imagined how young hoplites or Romans must have felt their first time in either a phalanx or a legion, standing shoulder to shoulder with other raw recruits.

The island was beginning to come alive and I heard one of the most distinctive and ever present sounds on Parris Island: yelling. I heard the cacophony of many hundreds of young warriors screaming at the top of their lungs. It echoed like the crashing of artillery in the distance that I would hear years later in the valleys of Afghanistan. It thundered in the distance, adding to the effects of chaos and evil that seemed to eradiate from the Island's sands. "*What were they saying?*" I wondered.

I attempted to decipher these foreign sounding commands and answers. I wondered if my platoon would one-day sound that same way. Admittedly, I was envious at all this yelling. I wanted to join them in their training. However, I did not earn that right just yet. After all, I was only a young recruit with a shaved head wearing bright red Nautica shirt and tan khakis. Everything on the island had to be earned. I became a tenant who paid my rent to the island in the gallons of sweat, screams, and pain that I would endure.

In terms of Marines, I was barely born into this world. Instead, I was a baby and I crawled along the floor. I didn't even earn the right to wear the cammies (battle dress utilities) that the other Marines and recruits were proudly displaying on their bodies as they boldly carried their rifles.

It was obvious I was daydreaming as SSgt Gomez asked me the question, "What??? Am I boring you, recruit??"

I had a planned response, "No Sir."

"Then get your friggin eyes back on me and listen up. When

I say 'forward march' you step forward with your left foot, and swing your arms." The impromptu drill instruction continued.

FIRST BREAKFAST

"RIGHT FACE! FO WARD MARCH! Lo Riiight! Haft Riite! Lo Riiite, Haft Right."

The Drill Instructors and many Marines pronounce the words "left" and "right" a bit different in order to ensure they maximize volume in their commands. We began moving to SSgt Gomez's confident commands. It would be a far cry to call what we were doing as marching. But it was an attempt.

"Rosy fingered" dawn began to touch the sky with light on my march. An epic and surprising beauty began to be painted across my eyes for me. Have you ever watched the land take shape under a sunrise? Most people never take the time to. However, it is an especially beautiful and spectacular event to behold.

A collage of new images was presented before me. It was a new world full of formations composed of well-disciplined Marine recruits, marching proudly with their rifles. I was mesmerized by their discipline as they slithered past my haphazard gaggle. I caught a glimpse of one of them as they passed us by. The recruit was a brilliant specimen, whose muscles and sneer was undoubtedly as a result of weeks of Marine Corps training. He broke his stare for only a moment and let out the subtlest of grin as he stared at us like the pathetic sheep we were. They glided past us as if they were Hell's honor guard to the rhythmic marching cadence of their Drill Instructor.

"Lo Rite, Luft Rite. Luft, Rite."

My platoon continued the slow gaggle toward the chow hall.

The tall oak trees and their Spanish moss seemed very out of place. It was my first time seeing moss of this sort. The moss seemed to tell you that Parris Island was not hell, but rather of this Earth. Visions of Huckleberry Finn ran through my head. However, visions of boyhood innocence were stricken from my thoughts as the first rays of dawn showed upon my brow.

It was not even 0530 yet, and the heat began to bore down upon my head, radiating like a campfire. *"Fuck,"* I thought to myself. *"This place is going to be hot as shit."* We continued the march and arrived at the chow hall.

"Platoon, Halt!" my Drill Instructor shouted. "Now listen up! Get in there, eat, drink a lot of water, keep your mouth shut, and get out. Is that understood?"

"Yes sir!"

"I can't hear you!"

"Yes Sir!" The platoon echoed.

The platoon filed into the chow hall, one recruit at a time. I remained locked at the position of attention, waiting for my file to move forward.

"Ears!"

"Open Sir!"

"When you go in my chow hall, you will hold the tray like this. Grab the tray with your hands and hold it against your chest until you are ready to receive your food. When you are ready to get your food, place it on the ramp and keep a hold of it. When you sit your tray at the table, go grab a glass of water and carry it like this. One hand covers the top and the other holds the bottom. Do you understand?"

"Yes sir!"

We had been there for only six hours and the training encapsulated each moment of time we were in there.

This was not my regular chow hall as I would later join 1st Battalion. This dining facility was in 3rd Battalion's area.

I entered the chow hall with the disorientation one has while visiting a restaurant in a different country. I was unsure of the customs of this place, or if I would even be welcome here. A strange foreign language of sorts graced my ears with cryptic phrases such as, "By your leave, sir!" Or "Aye Aye, Sir!" I was still wearing my civilian attire and the other recruits stared at me as if I was a virgin in a whorehouse. I felt them staring at us as we gathered our food, nervously and without confidence.

Finally, I had my tray in hand and went about the task of getting food from a cafeteria line. Having just come from high school, this task did not seem horribly foreign to me. However, as with all things on the island, even this became a new and stressful experience.

Recruits near the end of their training cycle were serving the chow, saying short phrases such as, "Stay motivated, recruit!" I looked upon these recruits as if they were the inhabitants of this modern day Spartan agoge. They seemed to grin at me and my mates still wearing our clothes from home.

One of the servers asked me, "Grits, recruit?" I had no idea what in God's name grits even was. As if not to anger my foreign host, I sheepishly answered "Yes."

I brought this new dish of corn kernels to my table and ate of it. It was my last meal wearing civilian clothes on the island. It was almost too fitting to partake of this southern meal here in what is a cauldron for turning the raw iron of men into a sharp blade necessary for taking life on the battlefield.

I sat down and enjoyed what was perhaps the most antisocial meal of my life. Meals, for most people, are very social events. It's typically a time to reflect and simply enjoy being alive. However, in the Marines, eating time is exactly that. This time is only used for taking in calories, so that you can be trained for the labors of chaos. The recruit that sat across from me gave me a look, which confirmed that we were both thinking the exact same thing. We were both wondering what in God's name did we get ourselves into.

There, while attempting to take in my meal, I was still attempting to make sense of the surrounding chaos that surrounded me like a storm on the Pacific. I was surprised to see desserts available in the chow hall. Such pleasurable food just seemed out of place here. Cakes adorned with whipped cream resonated a life and a freedom long left behind.

The meal was over within ten minutes and SSgt Gomez was helpful in reminding where on earth I actually was.

"You're done, 84! Grab your tray and get out of my chow hall."

With that came the end of my first dining experience in the world renown dining halls of Parris Island.

I found my formation outside and my Drill Instructor was again dressing 1084's sloppy lines.

"Eyes front! Thumbs along your trouser seams."

Utilizing my peripheral vision, I looked at this random collection of raw recruits that I was a part of. 1084 stood out like flamboyantly multi colored peacocks in its civilian clothes; especially set against the uniformed SSgt Gomez who held 1084 at the halt while the more senior recruit platoons proudly marched past.

"Don't move! Let them pass by. You're are not fit to even look at them yet."

I stood in awe of them. These muscular Marine recruits that passed us as if they were the Spartans themselves, with their polished boots, pressed uniforms, and unwavering rifles held at smart port arms. They marched stoically like moving redwood trees, and here my platoon wavered like river reeds in a windy storm.

"Would I ever get that far?" I wondered to myself.

The path was now clear and 1084 marched to the supply building. I marched in the middle of the formation and wondered what the formation must have looked like from the outside. It was like attempting to see the entire beast while only being in the intestine of the wolf. Military formations are controlled and protected by several different things. Sometimes, they are drill, raw intimidation, and weapons. However, other times they are something much more different than one would think. Men wearing large orange vests protect military formations, particularly those on training bases. We call them "road guard" vests.

These brightly colored vests or belts follow warriors throughout their military careers. They reappear time and time again during large unit runs and humorously even show up on bases in war zones. These glowing monstrosities appear as hilarious reminders to state that warriors are dangerous to one another. In some respects, wearing such bright vests or belts must be done. Troops sometimes behave like steer whose horns are shaved, so they do not hurt one another in the holding area.

1084 arrived at the clothing facility and came to a halt at this new place. SSgt Gomez called a halt and my platoon sloppily made a left face. In the distance, distant shouts sounded over in the distance.

"I cannot believe that such places still exist here in the modern world. Is this place even for real? What in God's name did I get myself into?"

Recruits ask themselves such questions over and over throughout training, and dozens of times an hour during the first day on the island.

Methodically and without emotion, the supply clerks issued uniforms, boots, and shoes. In the final years of the 20th century, Marine recruits were still issued the classic BDU uniforms adorned with the green, brown, and black shades of the wood-lands of North America and Europe upon them. The recruits tried on their boots and running shoes. I took my time in this method, as I knew that my feet would be as important for surviv-al as my rifle on this god-forsaken island.

Pants were no longer pants. Rather, they were called trousers. The uniform tops were not longer called shirts. Ironically they were called blouses.

"I don't care what you dressed like as a civilian, you will look sharp in my Marine Corps uniform," one of the supply Marines shouted.

The pounds and pounds of gear was collapsed into green duf-fle bags, which bore the new name of "Sea Bags." Carrying the issued burdens, 1084 made its way back to the receiving barracks. The beds in the squad bay looked terribly comfortable. However, there would be no time for sleeping, not just yet.

Each one of us was given a cardboard box. "Place your civilian clothes in these," SSgt Gomez ordered.

I shed the final remnants of my civilian self into this box. I stripped down and became naked before my mates. I packed up my civilian clothes, shoes, and sealed them up, like the final rem-nants of my civilian self. *Farewell innocence.*

Fare thee well innocence
Of kissing young girls in the fields
Of being late to school
Of leaving work without permission

Fare thee well late nights with friends

Good-bye mom and dad
And good-bye to my child-like soul

I must learn to hunt man
To ignore pain
To become violence and fear.
Go to bed my civilian self.

I will see you again.
Even if it is only for a brief while

I wore the camouflage uniform issued by the United States Marine Corps, or what we called cammies. Camouflage, to many, seems like just a uniform that soldiers wear. Some people choose to make fashion statements by camoflauge. Others think it is cute to dress their children in such attire. However, warriors know better.

Predators wear camouflage so they can efficiently stalk and slaughter their prey of choice. Warriors do this as well. Warriors resemble the color and shadows of the Earth, so that they may close with and rob the enemy of their lives. The Marines taught to come close to the enemy as riflemen; they must stealthily stalk him and come to 500 meters or less. Here warriors may hurl lead toward him and spill his blood upon the ground. Warriors are good friends with the earth as we only wish to fertilize it with the blood of vanquished enemy.

The sun was climbing higher on this first day in hell and the beds looked even more inviting than before. There would be no rest for 1084 until later that day. We merely stowed the equipment and locked the sea bags to the racks.

I never realized how tired I was until I was unable to rest on my own time. Here, the beds looked as inviting as an ice-cold Gatorade on a hot summer's day. The time to decide when to rest for myself was long gone. The Marines would now decide if and when recruits would be afforded a rest.

MOMENT OF TRUTH

Swiftly and with intensity, 1084 was assembled outside the barracks. The recruits marched to another administrative building whose name has faded into the dust of my memory. SSgt Gomez moved us into a large waiting room. Each man sat down, doing his best not to fall asleep. I have never sat in a chair in a waiting room and almost fell asleep in my entire life. At least, not until that day. I think this was nearly the most exhausted I have been in my life, up to that point.

To those that are warriors, sleep is not a right; rather it is a privilege. One learns to get it while you can. Warriors learn this lesson swiftly when they go to war. Fighting men balance their sleep between guard shifts and missions. It is a critical portion of morale and of mission effectiveness.

I waited in what looked like a waiting room in a hospital. I attempted to sit up straight and not dose off, like so many of us were. I sat there adorned in the foreign camouflage uniform; the color of which I had only worn previously during hunting excursions. The platoon escort, SSgt Gomez continually reminded 1084 to drink water and not to touch their faces.

My turn came up and I entered a small office manned by a very professional looking Marine.

"Sit down, recruit," he said.

He looked at my record and back at me. "Your record looks clean. Is there anything else you should tell me, before your background check goes through?"

I was a good kid in high school. I had excellent grades; played sports, and stayed away from partying, something the Marines would later teach me in my career. My first and only time getting drunk in my life up to that point was in Panama City Beach, during spring break of my senior year of High School—only a few months previous.

"No Sir." I replied.

"Are you sure?"

"Yes sir."

Although, I had nothing to hide, the Marine made me feel as nervous as if I was smuggling two kilograms of Columbian grade cocaine under my uniform.

Reading this scene, it may seem like simple protocol and routine. Before you go on any further reading this, you must realize that nothing is routine on Parris Island. Everything is done with intensity. Nothing is simple. You do everything as hard as you can. You exist in a maelstrom of chaos that any man or woman that has earned the right to wear the Eagle, Globe, and Anchor will never forget. These lessons, even early on Parris Island, were not so you could earn the uniform. Rather, they were to ensure your mind and body could survive to be a Marine.

The matter was soon concluded and I waited with the rest of my fellow recruits to complete their impromptu interrogations. Soon, 1084 was again corralled into formation, fed, and returned to the barracks. Following the evening meal, all the recruits wanted to do was sleep. Most of the troops were awake for nearly 40 hours now. The desire for sleep numbed some of the fear of the unknown in this mysterious island.

SSgt Gomez gathered the recruits in the temporary squad bay. He demonstrated the very important ceremony of how to properly make a military "rack" or bed. After 30 minutes or so, the recruits memorized this intricate dance pattern involving a "fart sack", sheets, pillowcases, and a green blanket. We were released to our racks and assisted our bunk mates. We worked together, he and I. This other nameless ghost with a baldhead wearing camouflage.

Everything is done by command on the island and individual actions are kept to a minimum. The platoon was instructed to get into PT (Physical Training—T-shirt and shorts) gear and shower shoes. SSgt Gomez moved us like cattle into the "head" for nightly hygiene. I looked at myself in the mirror and barely recognized myself. However, my glance would be short lived. 1084 was given only sparing time to shower, shave, and to brush their teeth. I didn't care about what I looked like. I just wanted to get to sleep for the night.

Order is maintained at all times on the island. This draconian code is enforced by not only the Drill Instructors, but by the recruits themselves. Before dismissing us to sleep, SSgt Gomez read aloud the fire watch roster. The watches were set in 60 minute intervals and those picked for the guard shifts were selected by an alphabetical roster. I was spared that duty on the first night.

COUNT OFF

The recruits of 1084 assembled on the bright yellow line, which ran the entire length of the squad bay. There were two yellow lines separated by about four feet which created the "Drill Instructor highway." The recruits faced one another, staring blankly over the heads of the recruits across the line. I stood at the position of attention with my money valuable bag, at the time a small blue canvas bag, which was about the size of a hand. Within it was any important belongings such as ID cards and credit cards, etc.

The recruits extended their arms in front of their bodies and

held them steady. "Count... off." "1, 2, 3,4, 5, 6, 7, ...12,13, 16."
Someone had messed up the count up.

"Alright recruits, drop into push up position."

We were given one more slight punishment.

Again we tried. "Count off." Said SSgt Gomez.

"1, 2, 3, 4, 5...65, 66,...95, 96, 97." Sir! The count on deck is
97 highly motivated recruits." 1084 of course did not have the
proper amount of intensity required of highly motivated recruits
and the platoon was ordered to sound off a few more times until
it had achieved the proper blood curling volume.

"Prepare to mount!" Each man moved to his rack. "Mount!"
I made it. I thought to myself. I laid down at the position of attention in my rack. I had the bottom of the bunk beds. I stared at
the top, as the lights were shut off. No one talked to one another,
as the men were too exhausted to even make pleasantries. I laid
there staring into the dark unsettling calmness that only a military barracks can provide. I listened to the boots of the roving fire
watch. My eyes closed without any orders and I drifted off into
that darkness known as sleep.

I awoke briefly at around 1:00 a.m. Opening my eyes, I reminded myself where exactly on earth I was. The moment embod-
ied silence apart from the soft steps of the roving fire watch. Moving my body to the side of my rack, my bare feet hit upon that cold
smooth floor which seemed to resonate within all squad bays in the
Marines. I soon found my shower shoes and made my way to the
head. I felt somewhat awkward as I was only wearing my brown
T-shirt tucked into my tighty whiteies or what we called skivvies.

I made my way to the head, passing a few more sacrificial
lambs on my way in. I relieved myself and moved to wash my
hands. This time, I took a few moments to stare at myself. I did
not recognize my bald self. I thought I looked somewhat hand-

some bald and touched my face. I came closer and looked into my eyes. I took a few deep breaths and stared into the inner depths of my soul and myself.

God, I hope I am doing the right thing.

I stared deeply into the mirror for perhaps two minutes, but it felt much longer. I was alone for few moments, in the quintessential womb of the Marine Corps. It was soothing to wash the warm water over my head in the silence. As I washed, I also hoped that some of my fears would wash off me and fall down into this drain. Training had not even started yet.

However, any man or woman that has stepped foot on this island can feel its power radiating from its buildings, concrete, and the very soil itself. It was this fear which always seemed to permeate the air I breathed, the water I drank, and the food I ate.

I had been on the island for roughly 24 hours and I could sense the magic and brilliance of this archaic modern day Spartan *agoge*. Here, I would find myself, like all warriors do. Here, I would ask myself, "Why?" Like we all do. Here, I learned to feel fear, then later ignore it, and even later make it into something even more useful. Fear was the Marine Corps pollen. Marine recruits tirelessly collected and transformed this prize into a honey composed of primordial anger, violence, and energy. One can see this ferocity in the eyes of any Marine, regardless if he is fresh off the parade ground at graduation or well into his 60's.

A few more recruits entered the head, interrupting my peaceful meditation. I met a few of their distant, groggy, and disoriented gazes. With a sigh, it was time for me to return to my rack. I moved back to my rack, closed my eyes, and drifted back to this safe, comfortable, peaceful sleep.

LIGHTS, LIGHTS, LIGHTS!

I have experienced few things more shocking to me than waking up Marine Corps style on Parris Island. I have woken up dozens of times to the sound of machine gun fire in Afghanistan. However, being awakened by these demonic seeming Marine Drill Instructors was by far more stressful. The awakening foreshadows and embodies the very element of chaos. These very same elements engulf the island to this very day.

The ceiling lights flickered on and with it my eyes slowly creaked opened. For a brief moment, time itself seemed to pause and the place was void of sound. The Drill Instructors came in screaming: "Lights! Lights! Lights! Get on line! Get on line! 5,4,3,2,1, Zero!"

"Freeze, Recruit! Freeze!" 1084 replied. The term "Zero" meant that all movement ceased and everyone was immediately quiet. The recruits took up positions again on the sacred yellow lines which ran the length of the squad bay. The men held their positions, locked like statues set in stone, at attention. The recruits stood there in tan shirts tucked into skivvies. One might feel a little awkward had this taken place anywhere else on the face of the Earth. However, here on Parris Island, there was no time or energy to point out something such as humor. There was only survival which came from obeying the next order as fiercely, swiftly, and powerfully as possible.

Almost nothing on Parris Island is done in the absence of chaos. Simple tasks in my former life became chaotic tests of courage, endurance, and strength. Something as simple as getting dressed was instantly transformed into a test of stress resistance and teamwork.

"Get your left sock on. You got 5, 4, 3, 2… Get your right sock on! You got 5, 4, 3, 2… Get your trousers on! You got 5,4,3…. Get your blouse on!" My Drill Instructors screamed. This phenomena continued throughout the entire time on the island; save graduation week.

That first time getting dressed on the island was one my most stressful times on the island and in my military career. Inevitably one of the recruits decided that he would attempt to get dressed out of sequence with the rest of the platoon. This individual slip of obedience was quickly suppressed.

"Zero! Oh good, someone wants to be an individual. What's your name recruit?" The stunned manned answered nervously. "Take everything off and throw it on the deck! You have 10,9,8,7...."

I stood there bare bodied to include my socks; leaving my feet exposed on the cold squad bay floor. It was my first of many times standing naked at the position of attention during my time on the island. The Marines have absolutely no tolerance for the disobeying of a direct order. Regardless if an infraction was intentional or not, it was punished in the manner one would blasphemy in medieval times. A misbehaved recruit was treated as if he had burned a picture of the Virgin Mary in St. Peters Church in Vatican City on Christmas Eve.

The Marines teach and ingrain this within its service members for many reasons. The Marines are America's shock troops. They are constantly called upon to participate in fierce battles, with at times questionable orders plunging them into danger. In battle, there is not time for hesitation, such things can put your comrades in danger and cost life.

Undressing was one of many lessons in order to teach the meaning of orders and of authority. The point was made—for the time being anyways—and the Drill Instructor dressed us.

"Get your left sock on! You got 5, 4... Get your right sock on!

You got 5, 4, 3…" The chaos continued and 1084 was eventually fully dressed.

Everything I did on the island was supervised to the most finite detail. I made my rack; ensuring I tightened every single loose inch of blanket and bed sheet. SSgt Gomez inspected and seemed to be everywhere at once. These Drill Instructors were master craftsmen in the art of making Marines, and nothing went unnoticed. Any recruit seen slacking off or even perceived of doing so was severely punished.

With the morning tasks accomplished, 1084 moved outside into the darkness and assembled into the tight platoon formation. The recruits looked sloppy as compared to the rest of the recruits on the island as our trousers remained unbloused. This morning, 1084 marched a bit better to breakfast, but it was haphazard at best. My platoon was fed with the same intensity and speed as before. I was and am still at awe as to how horribly efficient the Marine Corps is at accomplishing tasks. The sheer speed they could feed and water nearly 100 men was impressive.

I did not know what to expect next in this sideshow of chaos. That was the thing on Parris Island. One simply did not know what to expect next. *Where in God's name were they marching us to?*

"Platoon… Halt!" SSgt Gomez ordered. The first rays of sunlight began to light the Earth as 1084 halted just outside a red brick building whose perimeter was dressed with a fence complimented with razor wire. To an untrained new recruit's eye, it was not obvious that this was in fact an armory.

I met my companion who remained at my side throughout my entire time on the island: my rifle. I stood in silence, as always at the position of attention, in wait for my introduction with my dark steeled mistresses, with whom I learned to slaughter my foe on the field of battle.

The M16 A2 was thrust into my hands. I repeated the serial number loudly and sharply, G349507. She assisted me in earning my title Marine and prepared me for the battles I would fight years later and thousands of miles away. I never handled an assault rifle before that moment in time. The bolt was locked to the rear, and I had no idea how to close it.

Leaving the armory, SSgt Gomez looked at my rifle as he did to all the recruits. He slammed the bolt forward on my rifle and looked into my eyes without uttering a single word. Although I had always hunted and carried guns for years; this one seemed as a foreign object. I felt the power and aura of the other Marines that had slept with this piece of steel.

Every Marine is a rifleman. To the Marines, this is not merely some cheesy slogan to merely make people feel important. Rather it is a horrible truth. By graduation, every Marine — man or woman — possesses the skill set to take an enemy combatant's life at 500 meters. The rifle becomes a part of your warrior spirit. A Marine recruit becomes more intimate with this piece of steel than any woman they will have in their lives. This rifle was the key to graduation and, more importantly, it would become the key to survival on the field of battle.

1084 formed up and marched back to the barracks. I secured my equipment and rifle to my rack utilizing a steel cord that reminded me of the kind that I used to lock up my bike in junior high. Securing the rifle was, in itself, a process. I had to lock the bolt to the rear, and place the charging handle back into its seat. With this complete; I hung the rifle upside down, and utilized it's sling to hang on the post of my rack. The steel cord was wrapped through the open ejection port and secured with a combination Master Lock.

The sloppy pack of raw recruits was then herded to the medical center for initial shots and dental exams. It was the calm in some respects before the horrible storm that each one of us knew loomed just over the horizon. I snuck in what little small talk with the other recruits; when my DI masters were out of visual or audio range. I took the time to enjoy a bit of peace and to work out what exactly I had gotten myself into, a puzzle that I would constantly go over in my head.

I was near-sighted as a young man before I later receive PRK surgery in my twenties. I was fitted with those glasses of horrible legend — Birth Control Glasses or what we call BCGs. These glasses, as grotesque in appearance as they were, were very sturdy. I would bet money that their frames could resist a shot from a shotgun. These glasses were horribly uncomfortable at first. However, in time and with enough other things to worry about on the island, you learned to ignore them. Like my rifle, uniform, and everything else Marine, they became a part of me.

I was also given a strap for the glasses that the Drill Instructor affectionately called a "Brain Strap." With the medical screenings complete, 1084 was fed, watered, and returned to the barracks.

INITIAL STRENGTH TEST

The recruits were medically deemed fit to train and now 1084 had to prove that they could survive physically on these horrible drill fields. The initial strength test was composed of three events to test strength as well as endurance. These requirements were only basic and those who only could merely pass these events would suffer horribly throughout the training. The requirements were: 4 dead hang pull-ups, 50 crunches in two minutes, and a

1.5 mile run in 14 minutes. By graduation, each Marine was able to laugh and chuckle at such absurdly weak requirements.

The beauty of the Marine Corps training program is that it did not require a recruit to be an Olympic athlete to enter. Yet, those who were born of this fire and survived could endure the most horrible conditions with little complaint. The strength of the Marine Corps is not that they in make super human athletes (although some arguably are). One of the true strengths is that Marines believe that they are, in fact, super human. It is this belief that permitted them to win the unwinnable battles of the past, and continues to serve them in the battles of the 21st century.

I ensured that I could run three miles in under 20 minutes, do 10 dead hang pull-ups, and perform well over 100 crunches in the allotted two minutes. My body, if nothing else, was ready for this epic summer of pain and self-discovery.

I changed out of my camouflage uniforms and into my PT uniform. I wore a tan T-shirt, green shorts, which seemed too short for my liking, and my issued New Balance running shoes. 1084 again assembled into the 21st century phalanx and held at the position of attention, awaiting orders. There were over 100 young men in the ranks. Now, wearing only T-shirts, it was noticeable that some of the recruits were not physical specimens.

Those who failed the Initial Strength Test, were sent to the Physical Conditioning Platoon. This was also called the "Pork Chop" platoon by Drill Instructors; as they warned us of our fate should we fail this upcoming test. I had been on the island for less than 72 hours and had decided that 13 weeks would be quite long enough here. Those who were sent to the Pork Chop platoon could look at a total of 16-20 weeks or so on the island.

The South Carolinian heat was still beaming down upon my platoon as the hour approached late afternoon. I was only standing and the sweat trickled down my face. The little discipline that I had learned thus far prevented me from wiping the sweat out of my eyes or even licking the salt from my upper lip.

The time had come and the commands: "Right… Face; Forward… March" were issued by SSgt Gomez. It was a short march, and I was eager to release some of my tension during the upcoming workout. 1084 halted upon a large grass field adorned with pull-up bars, a track, and other devices for physical conditioning. Roughly a thousand young men formed up. I smiled at the scene and silently wondered if this was what the Roman Legions first resembled while they were being raised on a marshalling field on the Italian peninsula.

The thought of the Romans to this day makes me think at almost how absurd it is that my country must continue to train forces of men to slaughter the men of other countries. Warfare seems like such an archaic thing, and growing up comfortably in the suburbs of Detroit, it was difficult to imagine that such marshaling fields were still necessary to destroy others. It was difficult to imagine that such hatred existed in the world. Would men that I never before met truly try to kill me one day in battle? One day I would find the answer to this.

Platoon 1084 moved toward the pull-up bars. The Marines offered us a demonstration of this event. Each pull-up had to be conducted from a dead hang and without utilizing any forward momentum generated from swinging, or what marines called "kipping." The recruits broke into single file lines behind pull-up bars of varying heights. I waited for my turn.

I was far in the back of the line. From my perspective, I could see some recruits flawlessly performing their required amounts. A few struggled to even knock out a single pull-up. The ones which were obviously overweight, fluttered like frying fish in their attempts to execute. I felt sad for them. The Drill Instructors, knew how to deal with them. They were swiftly removed from the field and instantly sentenced to a few more weeks on this hell on earth.

It was nearly my time to mount the bar and I carefully listened to the commands issued by observing Drill Instructors. A few recruits mounted the bar without first being ordered and were instantly ordered away to the back of the line. I did not want to be one of those sent away. Although I was confident in my upper body strength, I wanted to get this portion over and done with.

"Approach the bar. Mount. Begin." The Drill Instructor ordered.

I conducted my pull-ups slowly and with flawless form; not giving the DI any excuse to send me away.

"You're done, recruit." The DI said.

I moved out to the next waiting area in the heat and my sweat continued to run from my pores.

Crunches were by far a much easier event for the majority of the recruits. The recruits counted for one another. However, the DIs warned the men over the extreme punishments for anyone dumb enough to be an integrity violator.

"Ready …begin!"

My partner went first and finished without any difficulty. My turn came next and I finished in the same manner.

1084 moved to the track and prepared for the run.

"Alright, you have five minutes to finish any final stretching."

It felt remarkable to be able to simply move without any direct orders or intense supervision. It was my first chance to do so during waking hours. I limbered up my legs, which were accustomed to running from my years of cross country and track/field.

"You're done recruits! Get ready!"

The recruits assembled on the track, shoulder to shoulder. The familiar tension of pre-race jitters was a welcoming sensation to my muscles and breathing. I stared at the ground, waiting for the signal. With a whistle blast, we started. All warriors are intimately familiar with the calm before being unleashed on the field of battle. It's always there with you. I felt in those moments the way I did waiting to ambush the enemy and while I was waiting to be called up on a QRF Mission in Afghanistan.

I loved being let loose and felt as happy as a wild stallion who was released to charge carelessly upon the prairie with my mates. I only had to keep a good jog to finish in the allotted time. However, I didn't want to take my time in the event of an unforeseeable ankle twist or fall. I finished the run in just under 11 minutes.

After crossing the finish line, I moved back to my canteen that was prepositioned in my platoon's last staging area. I picked it up and joined what was called the wagon wheel for the cool down. Here, drenched in sweat, I drank water and walked in a large circle, allowing my heart rate to lower and for my body to cool down.

It was wonderful to walk in this circle unsupervised. A large digital clock reminiscent of my days of high school football cascaded the time before my eyes. More and more recruits crossed the finish line. As the time came closer to the limit, more of the huskier recruits came across the finish line. With only five seconds remaining, a few of the bigger fellows made it. I could hear a few of the Drill Instructors commenting on how much of a struggle it would be for those who were weak in the cardio arena to complete the training that lie ahead.

"Alright, recruits. Now your foot is in the door," SSgt Gomez said to us.

These words were utterly encouraging and increased my morale a great deal. A few motivating words can shimmer like a thousand suns to those who stride in the darkness without a glimmer of hope. Leaders must learn when to shine such light on the warriors placed under their command and when not to.

1084 marched back to the barracks. My head swelled with pride, dwelling from those few encouraging words from SSgt Gomez. I was in. Now, all I had to do was survive the next 13 weeks. For the moment, becoming a Marine was my ultimate goal in life.

1084 was not praised any further for its recent victory. Rather, the training continued. I entered the barracks, was ordered to strip, get my shower shoes on and wrap a towel around my waist. The showers were turned on. Every other shower was blasting with alternating temperatures of hot and cold. I was being introduced to what was called a PT (physical training) shower. 1084 was given a right face and marched into the head.

The Marine Corps simple and effective culture found solutions for everything. They were able to have 100 men shower in under five minutes. I simply removed my towel from my waist and walked in a circle under the showers. The shower was simply meant to wash off one's sweat and cool you off. It worked. 1084 was soon back online and got dressed again. Of course, it was done in standard Marine Corps fashion: "By the numbers." "Get your left sock on! You have 5,4,3… and so on."

1084 even managed to get fully dressed without having to strip down naked.

My platoon was fed its final meal during this nascent stage of training. My forming time was concluded. In the morning, 1084 was to be given to the actual Drill Instructors and training would truly begin. I fell to sleep that night in anticipation for the chaos, which was sure to come.

TRAINING BEGINS. PLT 1084

DAWN

I started my last morning in the receiving barracks to that horrible alarm clock of stress engendered by florescent lights, the banging of garbage cans, and the hellacious screaming of my Drill Instructors. These demons performed their duty as if they were Cerberus's spawn. The hellhounds guarded not the gates of Hades, but rather the sacred title of Marine. They would not allow the weak or unfit to pass through their gates. These muscular beasts guarded the passage and held the keys in between their razor-sharp fangs.

I stood with my fellow recruits at my station upon the yellow line. I stood and attempted to peer through the thick fog of chaos and drowsiness. The dogs continued their incessant barks. "Count off!" the DIs ordered. My hands rose parallel with my shoulders and my head snapped to the right. 1084 began the count completely down the line: "1, 2,3,4….. 96." There was 96 of us now. The hounds dressed 1084 by the numbers and the recruits turned to morning clean up.

My platoon was fed and quickly returned to the barracks. The entirety of my equipment was stowed into my sea bag and ALICE pack. I was ordered outside, carrying the full bulk of my gear. 1084 formed up in ranks under the heavy burdens. It was time to walk to the barracks that belonged to Platoon 1084, Charlie Company, 1st Recruit Training Battalion.

Charlie Company banner.

Typing the mere words brings sweat to my hands. The very words and numbers themselves possess such strong magic. The affects of the magical science of war there still hangs heavily in my heart.

The magical aggression inherent in Marine Corps culture is forever a part of a Marine. We all feel it from time to time. Even if you are not one of us, you may feel this magic if you would like. All you must do is piss off a Marine. I feel it from time to time, even now with the measured emotional skill set of an officer. Once the anger starts, there is no stopping it. Once it starts, it feels like a waterfall of fire pouring off your soul. This power flows from an incessant spring that drives the very nature of war and hatred itself. It enables us to slaughter our enemy on the field of battle without hesitation. It permits the Marine Corps to act like the dogs of Hell that they are.

1084 began the march in the light cast by the mid summer's dawn. Parris island was truly remarkably with its above ground pipe system, archaic wooden buildings, and Spanish moss hanging carelessly on its trees. My burden was terribly heavy, and I could feel its sheer force bury itself ever deeper into my shoulders. SSgt Gomez kept a smart and swift pace on the march. It was his last few moments with us. He fulfilled his duties of in processing us into this savage of pain, power, drill, and misery.

My march began to slow up a bit and for the first time in my life I set my eyes upon Charlie Company's barracks. This small patch of ground became sacred Earth to me for the remainder of my years of life.

1084 entered the squad bay for the first time as a Platoon. This place became my home within the forging inferno of war. Here I rested and hardened my body for the task of war. Here, I shed pounds of useless fat and liters of sweat. I howled like a blood lusted hound for my Marine masters. Here I was forged in the fires of chaos and emerged with the ability to harvest the lives of my chosen enemy with surgical precision and the sharpness of a Katana.

Like the blades used by legendary Samurai, I was folded and folded, over and over again. My weight and ability would be tested and balanced until they were perfect for the task of battle. My masters noticed every imperfection. They were expert craftsmen and accepted nothing short of perfection from us.

I entered the squad bay, not knowing what exactly to expect. I placed my gear down near my rack and stood at attention.

"What was next?" I wondered.

The very floor in the center of the squad bay could have opened and revealed the path to hell; and I would not have been overly surprised by this act of wizardry. I would have merely accepted it as a part of the training plan. In all actuality, it would have given this place more sense. I mean, what type of mortal could produce and maintain this sort of intensity for so long.

SSgt Gomez walked down the center of the squad bay for the last time with us. These receiving Drill Instructors, like him, had already served their time on the island working for at least a couple years training Marine recruits. This was typically their final duty on the island. He strolled the length of my platoon, correcting positions of attention for one last time. He had us assemble on toward the edge of the Squad Bay—near the "Classroom"—which was nothing more than the bare open space which spanned from the Racks to the DI hut, quarter deck, and head. Here we waited.

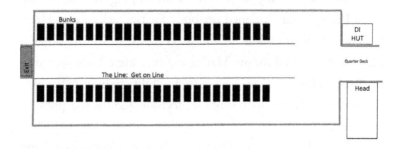

1084 sat rigidly, Indian style, in the same manner as they would later engage 200m and 300m targets on the rifle range.

"Left hand—left knee! Right hand—Right knee!" We yelled.

SSgt Gomez confidently yelled and asked: "Your backs are?"

"Straight, sir!" We screamed.

He asked again and we again screamed: "Straight, Sir!"

I sat there on the cold floor cooled by the barracks air conditioner. The artificially cooled air felt lovely as compared to the already sweltering South Carolinian summer air outside. I did my best to keep my back straight and erect. I fought the undisciplined civilian urge to adjust my posture or scratch my face. I concentrated on the task at hand — survive and obey. The silence was soon broken.

The Company leadership entered the squad bay. They marched smartly onto the quarterdeck, with precision that reminded me of the Marine Corps Silent Drill team from the commercials that I had seen about the Marines in years previous to this moment in time. My Company commander first addressed us. Marines of every rank, both officers and enlisted, are known for their professionalism. Parris Island was the example for all recruits to learn and to adhere to through their careers as Marines and in their lives for years for as long as their minds remain capable of preserving memory.

My Company Commander addressed us in the professional manner I came to expect of all Marine officers on the island and even now in my professional military life. He told us what we needed to hear, "We all could do this." At the time, I did not realize how genius and well thought out the Marine Corps leadership model was. I would later remember it as I prepared to take my own men into the fires of battle. In the face of uncertainty, chaos, and the uncertainty survival — it is essential to remind those that stand on the doorstep of Hell's circus that they all are capable of accomplishing this task.

Although, laconic in his rousing — his words did what I needed them to do. They told me that I actually could do this. They told me that I could actually do battle with these demons in smoky bear hats and not only survive but graduate as a United

States Marine. He then introduced us to some of the most influential men I would meet in my life: my Drill Instructors. He turned to them and gave the DI oath. He called forth my Senior Drill Instructor.

"Senior Drill Instructor! Take charge of your platoon and carry out the plan of the day." The commander said.

"Aye, Aye, Sir." SDI SSgt Telford replied.

The Senior Drill Instructor came forward with his own prepared statement. His words were calm, but fiercely confident. SSgt Telford wore the distinctive black belt around his waist, signifying his position as the Senior Drill Instructor. He stated again, that all the recruits were capable of completing this epic quest. However, he stated that he and every other Marine would only accept 110% from 1084, at all times. He then introduced the junior Drill Instructors who wore the distinctive Green belts with Golden buckles whose Eagle, Globe, and Anchors shined brilliantly.

CHAOS

A Marine's life cycle begins with a hurricane of shock, terror, and fear. Like the ancient Earth, Marines are created on a landscape of disorder, fire, and storms. In battle, Marines move toward the sound of guns and death itself. My time spent in the womb of Parris Island was what prepared me for horrors of war.

Those who have drunk of the strong wine of battle know that war is the epitome of chaos in the human experience. To fight for the mere right to breathe is a feeling that combat veterans hope their loved ones may never experience. Yet, in these mortal contests called firefights, riflemen and leaders alike must stand and ignore the human want for self preservation. In combat, warriors must look directly into the sun, although we know too well that our retinas could be being burned to a crisp. We stand here and do battle with the Devil and the horrors of hell.

Marines have a tendency to enter in the hottest campaigns and battles. Their history is etched in the most intense battles, ranging from Bladensburg, Beallau Wood, Iwo Jima, Khe Sahn, and more recently with names such as Falljuah or Marjah. Marines thrive in the fires of chaos, for they were raised besides these fiery embers. It is in battle, Marines do what they were designed to do.

A Marine does not experience hell in battle.

A Marine simply returns home.

In some respects, many of the recruits, including myself, were in fact lost souls, unable to properly function in the light of the civilian world. Many of the recruits sitting there cross-legged searched for something more from life. I know I did. I sought something different in life. I wanted something more than just my boring life of studies, sports, drinking, and girls. I grew tired of the shire.

Some of us who are warriors seek the other side. Some people study warriors and claim that they are all sick beings, who bring only terror and death to the world. Perhaps they are right. Regardless of how you feel about warriors and our horrible techniques of reaping the lives of mankind—we are that necessary evil.

Warriors are those horrible muscular Rottweiler's, people kept caged in the backyards of their peaceful suburbs. They are kept hidden away in the shadows—where by training they are forever tormented. They are teased with visions of glory and wining—but instead are tortured for years on end with forced marches, runs, extended field problems, and thousands of rounds of blank and live ammunition.

At times, they are released from the training cages and run carelessly alongside of the weak and selfish sheep. They drink, and fight too much on these Friday and Saturday night adventures. They return to their cages on Sunday, with the nocturnal adventures freshly documented still upon their heads in the form of hangovers.

Monday mornings come back sharply on runs or marches. Warriors are home again, in their small cages, I smile at my tormentors—even assisting them to help torment others within my pack.

There is one but only one relief from the Spartan and mundane lifestyle known as Garrison: War. In War, warriors are permitted to behave as the Rottweiler's that they were trained to be. Here, they leave the green fields of peace and trot upon the bloody deserts and valleys of war. Here, they may find prey, run them down, and end their pitiful lives in between their powerful jaws and razor sharp teeth. Warriors smile as they shake their small lifeless bodies in their jaws. They rip them into shreds with blood lusted rage to protect the sheep of our country. Warriors will give them pain and turn their bodies into piles of meat, blood, and bone. May they die.

I would become a Marine. I would become Chaos. I became death.

INVENTORY

The Marine officers, the Series and Company commander, marched away, moving gracefully like beautiful well-groomed stallions of men. They made sharp facing movements out of the squad bay. They left 1084 to the Drill Instructors and masters of my life for the next few months. Soon 1084 was alone with these demons of warriors.

The thing that makes a Marine recruit's time so terribly difficult is that first you have to imagine a world where all misery, pain, happiness, and rest comes not from one's own hands but rather from the hand of another man. These Drill Instructors were trained to keep you alive through this journey—however comfort and politeness were at the bottom of their priority list.

Only the enlisted Senior Drill Instructor and Green belts remained. These men stood there like colossal statues. Beautiful with their tan uniforms hanging from their toned and tanned instruments of war. They stood like some sort of deadly combination of Achilles and the statue of David. They stared into the vast sea of us shaved, frightful, and bald recruits. Without any flaws or empathy, they stood over us like muscular demons tasked with guarding hell's gates might look upon the helpless lost souls who have been cast down from heaven after receiving disapproval from St. Peter.

Time on Parris Island is magnified beyond belief or comprehension. Here, it seemed that one learned an entire encyclopedia of knowledge in only a few hours, days, and weeks. The educational genius of the Marine Corps is a thing to be studied and marveled at. My education into this world of terror and war was just beginning. I sat down in one of the many lectures in this Oxford of violence.

The next lesson on that fateful morning was that the Marine Corps could utilize any situation and make it as stressful as an amphibious assault on a heavily fortified beach. The Marines wielded power, stress, and control as the poet does with words; and these Drill Instructors were the Kiplings of their time.

The initial task given to the Marine Drill Instructors was to ensure that we had the proper gear to continue training on Parris Island. To the casual reader, it may seem that an inventory would be one of the easiest tasks a Marine recruit may encounter. Nothing could be further from the truth.

The shock and savage ferocity of that moment reverberates through every muscle fiber and bone in my body to this day. It is now apart of my soul and my entire being. I can recount it as if it was yesterday that I began my journey on this horrible savage training ground of war.

One of the hardest things about writing about traumatic episodes in one's life is, in part, reliving the moment. I have been reliving this proud but traumatic chapter in my life for years at a time. It reawakens those evil and primordial feelings. It feels like I'm walking over hot coals over one the greatest fires of my life.

Battles, whether you are lucky enough to initiate the contact, or more often than not as was the case for me in Afghanistan are on the receiving end, are initiated with a primordial shock laced by fear. It stings more than anything else on earth. This shock slaps you with the force of a thousand tidal waves. It ignites every animal instinct within a body and soul.

The shock of battle is nearly impossible to put into words or to replicate in anything short of mortal combat itself. However, in my years of training and interlaced with firefights, the Marines have discovered a method to replicate this fearsome and unholy experience. The Marine Corps has found that magic formula to replicate the feeling and intensity of battle. Like growing bacteria in a culture, the Marines have found a way to grow and utilize fear in this cell culture of Parris Island. To this day, I am still puzzled and revel at the pure efficiency.

GET ON LINE!

"Get on line! Move, Move, Move!"

This is one order that I, and all Marines, will never forget. This memory remains smoking now like a wild fire in the dark forests of my warrior heart.

I ran with the intensity in my muscles like I did running to one of my platoon's positions during battle years later in Afghanistan. However, I think the feeling felt graver there at Parris Island than in battle. We all ran within this human wave of fear, power, and intensity. The DIs ran at our feet; chomping like timber wolves chomping at the feet of a herd of helpless lambs.

I made it to my sacred spot on the line, turned around and did my best to become like stone at the position of attention. I successfully ran the 20 meters from my seated position to my spot on the line. However, the yelling did not stop. Here on this island there was always yelling. The noise amplified, both their orders and 1084's replies. The Drill Instructors told us that we were not yelling loud enough. I was sure that every man in that room was scared as shit and did his best. However, it did not matter. These wolves were in bloodlust and demanded more from 1084. They demanded fear, sweat, and perhaps our souls. Together, the recruits were lit aflame in this squad bay.

The very air seemed to flex with noise, sweat, orders, fear, and rage. The squad bay became alive. I never imagined or prepared myself that Parris Island would be this much of a shock. The devil himself could not prepare you for the dark magic.

"Do what you are told and you will be okay." The paternal advice given from my Recruiter in Michigan echoed through my ears. "*Okay, I can do this.*" I thought to myself.

I remained locked at the position of attention, remaining still as if I was in an ambush position. It was difficult not to look to my side, as the wolves continued their devastating attacks on the ranks. The noise is what really got me. I felt like I was a wildebeest standing in a herd, as another beast was being torn to shreds in full view of the herd. The DI's voices were powerful and confident. 1084's replies, were like that of dying herbivores on the African plain.

The chaos never ceased, but the noise did, but did so only briefly.

"At this time, turn your sea bags upside down and spill everything onto the deck in front of you. When I call for an item, pick it up, hold it in front of you, and place it back into your sea bag, when told so. Do you understand that?" The DI asked.

"Sir, Yes Sir."

"At this time, pick up six pairs of boot socks!"

"Sir, Yes Sir!"

The Drill Instructors counted down "5,4,3,2..." I frantically clawed through my pile of gear and uniforms to find these fucking socks. I clawed at the camouflage and was relieved with only one second remaining, I stand with my arms extended. Sadly, not all the recruits are lucky enough and are punished. 1084 was punished for its lack of intensity in the moment.

"Put it back down, too slow. When we give orders, that means now! Do you under stand that?" The DIs screamed.

"Yes sir!" 1084 replied.

"Mountain climbers go... push ups go..., side straddled hops go!" My

muscles burned and only loud breathing was heard after twenty seconds.

Sweat trickled down from my head and dripped down onto the deck. "Recover!"

1084 moved back to the position of attention, all the recruits sweating and panting.

"Too slow recruits! Back down. Push ups... go."

This continued for a few minutes longer. The entire time the wolves were relentless, growling horrible sounds to the weaker recruits and sometimes to recruits for no reason at all. When I was there in that moment, I felt that I was being tortured and these men were madmen. However, it was only years after, and following seeing war first hand, where the pure genius of the formula of producing a Marine comes to light.

There on the floors, sand, and water of Parris Island men became more and more desensitized to the rigors of combat and stress. Once someone steps foot on the island, they arrive as raw iron ore. The island is a forge, where the impurities are heated and beaten out of a recruit. It is not an easy process. However, if one wants to be a sharp blade, you find a way to cope.

1084 was back on its feet.

"At this time, pick up four sets of trousers! Ready... Move!"

I tore through the pile quicker, as I did not want to be the reason for the platoon to be punished that time. The Marines found ways to point out that the failure of one man can spell disaster for the entire unit.

"At this time, pick up two shower shoes! Ready, Move!"

I found mine, quite easily as the pile was became smaller and smaller. Another recruit was not so lucky.

Recruit Star stood up with the rest of us when the countdown had ended. However, he stood without shower shoes.

Sgt Staley noticed this action and charged him like a blood-soaked male African lion running down a mangy and hated hyena on the savannah.

"What's your name RECRUIT!???" Sgt Staley roared at the young man.

"Recruit Star, Sir!" He replied with the look as if the Grim Reaper materialized in front of his death bed.

Sgt Staley hatefully stared at him, as if he forgot his rifle on a combat patrol. He growled incessantly at the young recruit with his powerful face, every muscles flexed and vein pumping oxygenated blood to his brain.

"Repeat after me 84! Thank you, Recruit Star!"

We reply, "Thank you Recruit Star!"

1084 was sent to the deck and smoked again and again. We were punished as a whole for the failure of one man. Years later in battle and in unnamed valleys across the earth, I learned the importance of duty. Yet, here I did not know it yet. The punishment continued. The windows bled with our sweat and our pitifully weak yells. The world was on fire.

"ON YOUR FEET!" The DI's yelled.

I stood at attention, unmoving, secretly in awe of the unfolding chaos that was engulfing my fellow recruits and me. I tried to keep my mouth shut as I desperately breathed in gulps of fresh air. The recruits stood there rigidly, like young saplings watching as a forest fire engulfed our surroundings. The DIs continued their rants, exuding raw power and confidence in each of their movements. The echoed screams of the Drill Instructors and recruits blended as one in this maelstrom of Death.

I felt a bit of relief as I noticed that my pile of gear at my feet was getting smaller and smaller. As brutal as these exercises were, I knew that they would not last forever. This one was almost done. Almost, but not quite yet.

The inventory continued. My platoon clawed for various items such as canteens and different parts of our kit.

One of the recruits at my side was too slow in gathering the necessary piece of gear. The Drill Instructor swooped down upon him like an eagle diving toward a salmon in a mountain river. I was in awe of this DI as he was disciplining one of my mates. I could see his sweat permeate through his tanned "Charlie" shirt. His veins were piercing out of his neck as he shouted. His yelling sounded more savage than anything I had ever heard in my life.

The screams and shouts soon faded for a few moments.

With the gear stowed, the Drill Instructors stated: "For a head call! (Marine for time to use the bathroom)." 1084 was marched into the head, as always with the rigidity, proximity, and control one came to expect while at Parris Island. The recruits moved in an unholy fashion like little more than stock cattle. The urinals were the large steel open tanks, with jets of water slowly cleaning out human waste. They were reminiscent of the large dance clubs of my youth.

For many people, utilizing the bathroom can be a very relaxing time. Perhaps, because we are forced to be alone. Being alone, especially in the 21st century, is a very peculiar thing. Are we ever truly alone? Technology seems to fill in that ancient human gregarious need and instinct. Social media forums keep us close and involved in everyone else's life, that is except for our own.

Yet, for many people, utilizing the bathroom, be it at work or at home, is a sacred time to be alone. It is a time where people may shut out the entire world and allow themselves to be those fat beasts of the field, pissing and shitting any unused food products. Here we sigh, and perhaps enjoy a magazine or perhaps more likely in the 21st century read the latest Tweets or status updates on Facebook.

On Parris Island, the most basic pleasures are prohibited on this modern floating Hell in the South. Even the bathroom stalls lie without doors. Recruits are obligated to take care of the call of nature in plain sight of each other. Initially, this experience was very awkward and I was bashful squatted in plain view. In time, this most basic human need became easier and easier, to the point of having quite normal conversations with other recruits as my curriculum in hell continued. Erich Remarque, in his book *All Quiet on the Western Front*, commented on this same issue. Warriors have no need for such ridiculous things such as bashfulness. Rather, they need each other.

1084 was transforming into a platoon. Recruits found unsuited for training were weeded out in the initial days of forming and at the Initial Strength Test. It was apparent now that training would soon begin and prepare me for this bloody profession. I was embarking on an adventure of a lifetime.

For me there was no going back now. Like many Marine recruits past, present, and future, I made the sacred oath to myself. I would get off Parris Island in either a body bag or as a United States Marine. I continually repeated my promise to myself at least a dozen times on my hike to lunch that day. I remembered it as I stood at attention, while the sand fleas drank of my sweat and dined upon my flesh. The recruits of 1084 holding the position of attention became a banquet hall to these flying beasts.

The first 96 hours of a Marine's experience are some of the most memorable he or she will ever have. The initial moments are designed to shock one clear of civilian life and introduce a world where the elements of pain, violence, chaos, obedience, and anger rein as Gods. Any Marine you will ever meet will be able to recall these opening hours of boot camp, as if he was an ancient bard who memorized the lines of the Iliad in Iambic pentameter. Marines will forever remember their war song. There is no getting away from it.

The tenets of shock, power, speed, chaos, and aggression were perpetually present during training, hanging there in the young recruits lives, like clouds in the summer sky. Every action a recruit carries out from the first waking moments in the squad bay, to taking a piss, to finally going to sleep at night is strictly dictated by cult-like rituals. Recruits are ruled by these Gods and severely punished by their guardians in Smokey bear hats and form fitting uniforms. Ironically, the only escape one is given from these laws is when you are no longer controlled but unleashed in the arena of chaos.

I was provided some relief when I joined in mock battle, such as an obstacle course or a run. Or when I was unleashed and ordered to charge at another recruit as if it was the battle between Achilles and Hector on the plains of Troy.

I began to accept the chaos. I started to become all things that make fear.

PHASE I

DRILL

The first few days of training on Parris Island melted together like pieces of steel welded by a stream of lava. The training schedule was made up of chow, PT, drill, chow, classes, drill, PT, chow, drill, and sleep. Like the background of birds chirping in the forest, there was never an absence of chaotic yells from the Drill Instructors who continually tempered the recruits in the hellacious flames of war. Parris Island is the center and the origin of War. It is the forge of Mars.

Drill is one of the essential foundations for the Marine Corps and the Western military tradition. These carefully choreographed formations have served as the platform for effective fighting formations of successful western armies since the time of Rome's Legions, to linear Warfare, and even to modern day. Drill takes cowardly individual men and molds them into tight fitting and aggressive fighting formations. Drill makes normal men into finely tuned instruments of war.

Drill can spread fear onto observers of it. From the Persians watching the Greeks march upon the plains of Marathon, to the American continentals watching their British opponents slowly close the distance with bayonets drawn at the ready. Drill holds the secrets to many things in the art of war. These movements take the thinking out of normally what are highly complex movements. Drill permits warriors to ignore self preservation and reap men on the plains of war.

The closest thing that I did to Drill prior to join the Marine Corps, were my techniques performed on the floor of my Karate Dojo. Learning marching was as foreign as learning a different language. However, the importance of this western martial practice cannot and must not be underplayed.

The Drill Instructors were relentless in their efforts in teaching us. A well drilled platoon would march fearlessly into the gates of hell, as long as a DI called the cadence. Drill has the ability to shape regular men into beasts of war. I learned to be deadly in my movements and utilized attention to detail. Drill is one of the most important elements in the creation of a Marine.

I remember watching a platoon that was on the cusp of graduating. Watching a platoon of recruits close to graduation is like watching a formation of Grim Reapers synchronized with pain and effort swimming in a pool filled with blood shed from the millennia of battle. They marched like a moving phalanx of death, gliding effortlessly on the hot asphalt and sand on the island. They moved to the command of their warlords and followed any order he gave with razor sharp obedience and effectiveness. They were beautiful, powerful, and extremely menacing.

Initially, 1084 marched sloppily and without cohesion, as is always the case with rookie platoons. The movements, to me, initially felt awkward and I bounced in my steps. It would be weeks later that my Drill Instructors taught the platoon to flex our gluts during marching to hold us steady in our movements.

Recruits arrive to the Drill Instructors; raw and in need of sculpting. I began this training as an unshaped block of granite covered with moss. The Drill Instructors are experts in both their verbal and physical chiseling techniques. Each day, regardless if 1084 was on the physical training field, the parade ground, the classroom, or the squad bay, the recruits were chiseled by the Drill Instructors. Every imperfection that prevented young men from being wonderful instruments of war was hacked away by the Drill Masters.

My first week on Hell's parade grounds were unforgettable. Attention to detail was stressed into every joint and muscle. 1084's first drill sessions involved the Drill Instructors moving up and down the ranks screaming corrections with the utmost dire. These Drill Instructors injected combat enthusiasm into these peacetime exercises. They screamed in the manner that a squad leader would yell at a machine-gunner, in event that the enemy was within meters of the wire. They screamed with a primordial hatred as if a recruit had fallen asleep while on guard in the Korengal valley.

"Port… Arms!"

One and Two.. I shout. I stand there, gripping my rifle in front of my body. Fuck… it's hot. I dare not move, not even to wipe away the rivers of sweat dripping down my body. There is only this moment alone. There is silence. No commands, but I dare not move. I hear him, walking the ranks amongst us. He is making corrections.

Please God, let my form hold…

I hold steady. The wolves continue to shout at the ranks. The air in the distance waves from the heat rising from the concrete of the drill field. There is nothing but this moment. I must own it. I only wait for the next command.

"Right Shoulder… Arm!" Forward… march!"

To the Marine Corps, there are few worse sins than disobeying a direct order. Whether this sin is intentional did not matter. As a Recruit on Parris Island, a mere mistake may seem just like that. We are like rookie artists or writers that believe that one can merely throw out their mistakes as bundled up pieces of paper into the trash.

However, in the school of warfare there are a few absolute truths. Mistakes can cost a warrior his sight, limb, or life. Something as small as forgetting to slap a magazine hard or double checking a grid coordinate can cost not only one's own life; but the lives of the men entrusted to a leader. The Drill Instructors strive to pound this into the recruits during their nascent state of warriors.

During drill, 1084 marched to the drumbeat of fear and aggression on the parade ground. The Drill Instructor's cadence rang incessantly in our heads: "Luft... Rite, Luft Rite... Luft..." 1084 began with simple movements such as order arms, port arms, column rights and lefts, mark time march, and halt.

The Drill Instructor method of correcting recruits was genius as it educated the entire platoon in addition to the actual recruit being corrected.

"Four inches from your chest while at port arms, Recruit Sanchez! Do you understand?" Drill Instructor Sgt Staley screamed.

I looked at Sgt Staley and stared at his veins popping out of his neck. Staley was African American, powerfully built, and had dark piercing eyes. He was a force to be reckoned with, and the recruits feared to be corrected by him in particular. In the deep South Carolina heat and laced in sweat, Sgt Staley looked like Shaka Zulu himself, unmatched by any bald and pathetic recruit.

Recruit Sanchez screamed at the top of his lungs: "Yes Sir!"

"No, you don't, do you Recruit Sanchez?? Sgt Staley screamed. "Yes Sir!"

"Oh ... so I'm wrong! Is that what you are saying?? Sgt Staley Screams.

"No Sir!"

It went on like this for hours, but the corrected recruits were different. At times, those needing extra instruction were moved from formations and corrected in plain audible distance from the rest of the platoon. These corrections were harsh and violent, but it ensured that one did not forget the lesson. On the parade ground, recruits were not being taught merely drill movements for a temporary span of time. Rather, the drill movements were forever tattooed into the warrior record of our mind. Ask any Marine, and his time on the drill field will be amongst his most vivid memories of Parris Island.

"Port Arms!" was called by SSgt Insco, who was as tough as any Drill Instructor. However, SSgt Insco was well into his 30's and looked like more of a father figure. He could still bring down the sting of hell when necessary; but he was not as fierce as Sgt Staley. I conducted each of the movements as best of my ability as possible. Every recruit did. There was one common problem within all the recruits, they were not yet United States Marines. They were nasty and undisciplined recruits.

I held each position as best as I could. Holding a position such as port arms was difficult while the wolves continued to walk up and down the ranks slicing up any minute flaw in the recruit's positions. They continually nipped at us. Shortly after a halt, a DI was sure to swoop in and scream like a demon fresh out of the gates of hell!

"That's right, Recruit Summers… Slime! That's what you think of this platoon, isn't it??!"

Recruit Summers at that point in the training was uncertain if he should answer or not. SSgt Insco was angered even further by this apparent lack of respect.

"Well what is it then Recruit? Yes sir, No sir, Fuck you sir! Something!"

Recruit Summers answers with the anticipated, "No Sir!"

My education continued, eternally it seemed, in the summer heat of Parris Island. 1084 drilled with 110% intensity; which was the only acceptable level of effort permitted out of a recruit while on the island. While the DIs were tearing into my platoon; I always had a sick feeling in my stomach. I constantly hoped and wished that I was not next. The thing was the DI gods always had my number and soon I would be trapped into their next educational lecture.

Corrections made by the Drill Instructors were always incredibly traumatic exercises. I have been in several fights in my life; short guys usually have that about them. I was no stranger to intensity. However, these episodes were something a bit different.

The Drill Instructors are teachers and good teachers always take the time to learn the names of their students. Luckily for Drill Instructors and unfortunate enough for a few of us; those of us who arrive at the island near-sighted are given two gifts: BCGs (birth control glasses) and a nickname. The first time that I realized this, I was educated just after making a mistake in my manual of arms. Sgt Staley educated me in this matter.

"Stop, Glasses! You are wrong!"

Sometimes my name was glasses, as were the rest of us who were given those cursive BCGs.

Sgt Staley placed his large hands in a knife hand before my face (insert picture). All recruits become intimately familiar with this pose and learn to realize that a sharp educational discourse would soon follow. Sgt Staley continued screaming at me in the intense filled array all recruits came to expect.

I answered by screaming the prepared programmed responses including: "Yes sir, No Sir, and Aye aye, Sir!"

While being corrected I often experienced a somewhat out of body experience with the Drill Instructors. I was there but was not. Strangely, these shockingly loud educational sessions give me the strange ability to hyper focus on a given task. I compare it to the ability of trimming a bonsai tree while blasting the song: "Let the bodies hit floor" at full volume.

I was different, as I found my greatest Zen moments in these supreme storms of chaos. These feelings of hyper focus Zen would later return to me over a decade later in the battlefields of the Pech River Valley, Kunar Province, Afghanistan.

This fascination for me came from my years in the Martial Art Dojo. There are few things more pure to a warrior than the song of combat. In combat, whether sparring, at the rifle range, or on the battlefield, you are forced to focus on the moment. A failure to focus can result in a bloody nose, a broken limb, or a lost life. I am at peace during such times. It is this sick meditation where warriors must find the eye of the storm. Sgt Staley saw me relaxing in this session of chaos I think; and became enraged. His shouts became ever more enraged and intense. His powerful hands extended his pointer finger from his right hand and moved toward my eye.

His finger moved with such force that I think that it could go straight through my eye and into my brain. I was not lucky, and I had to go on living in this sultry hell of mine. His pointer finger imprinted sharply on the lens of my sturdy BCGs. He continued to scream at me and I remained in my Zen warrior trance, attempting to shield myself from the fiery chaos of this place.

Sgt Staley stared directly into my eyes. I was smart enough to not dare to respond in this challenge. The DIs were like ravenous wolves and I knew it was horribly unwise to return the stare into this tempered warrior's gaze. Instead, I chose to stare at his forehead, not permitting his fearless eyes to meet mine. His yelling was nearly done and he grew tired of me, like a cat who is done tormenting a mouse. He moved on down the line to educate more of the lost souls.

His sweaty finger left a finger print planted upon my lens. It took every bit of discipline learned on the island thus far to not rip my glasses from my head and clean his fingerprint off. Instead, his fingerprint remained there for about an hour. I become lost in the many curves of his print which strangely resembled one of those mazes that I so enjoyed doing in the coloring books of my long-lost youth. It was funny to think of such an obscure innocent moment there on the training ground of war.

Drill continued in the squad bay of my barracks. We spent time in the hot sun for hours that day and were tired. The Drill Instructors were not loving mothers to us. However, they knew all too well the toll of the hot South Carolina sun. 1084 was moved to the barracks to continue the toil without the threat of passing out. The commands of the Drill Instructors continued and the recruits attempted to complete each movement in unison and with precision. 1084 failed at this task, of course, and the howls of the DIs correcting continued and maintained a murderous level of intensity.

I stared at his fingerprint. His fingerprint and the efforts of this man were forever imprinted upon my warrior soul and my memory. It has been nearly fifteen years since that lesson in that stuffy squad bay and his voice and face still ring loudly in the halls of my heart and spirit.

Drill for the day was finished and my platoon was permitted to make a head call. I walked into the head and waited for my turn to piss. I took my glasses off and wiped my lens clean with the bottom of my tan T-Shirt. I survived just one more day.

ON DRILL

Recruits never stop drilling for the duration of their stay on the island. Short of wearing combat gear; it never stops. The Marines treat drill as a sacred practice, like the Muslims during their daily prayers. We pray not to God in the marching worship. Rather Marines pray for victory in war. I continue to drill even now in my most secret and dark dreams. Any Marine can close his eyes and probably mentally, if not physically, demonstrate a manual of arms that would even impress the guards at the Tomb of the Unknown Soldier.

Marine recruits at the position of Port Arms.

Drill, to the modern observer, can appear as an outdated module of training. Especially, in the 21st century where training aids such as paint balls, lasers, and even fake blood can be thrown into the curriculum. I disagree to the thoughts of the outdated training module theory. Rather, I think that the simplistic direct obedience to orders that drill presents is more important than ever in the mayhem and speed of war in the 21st century.

Drill encapsulates the sheer power and ability a group of individuals possess once they give up solitary wants, pains, and desires. It is when they surrender their individualism for the something even more powerful than themselves that men may become true disciples of war. True warriors must give up all their petty wants for the strength of the formation. This is not a socialist point of view, not even close. Rather these are those rare concepts that are easily briefed in a power point slide or at some cheesy leadership conference; the words: **cohesion, teamwork, espirit de corps, sacrifice, valor, discipline**

These words, are just words. However, the sheer power that resides within such a list of words is nearly indescribable. Concepts such as these can explain the unexplainable in human military affairs. These words can explain the mass suicides at places that echo throughout history such as Luectra, Thermopylae, and the Alamo.

Such concepts can be briefed neatly on a power point slide or even presented in books such as this. However, a warrior knows that the meaning of words such as valor, sacrifice, or deprivation will never be learned in an air-conditioned classroom or while being read while sitting on a comfortable lazy boy. Rather, they must be earned. They are initially learned on those God-forsaken corners of the world such as Parris Island, MCRD San Diego, and Sand Hill. These lessons are further ingrained upon warrior's minds at exams at the world's testing centers known to us as Khandahar, Helmand, Falljuah, and Kunar.

PUGIL STICKS

Marines must learn to unleash violence to survive. They learn it toe-to-toe initially, with a Drill Instructor screaming in their face. Later, they learn how to employ it against one another. Recruits learn to make war upon one another.

Recruits are given lectures of violence in the most appropriate classrooms for a warrior: The Arena. These arenas were large circles ringed with old tires and filled with sawdust. It was here where we were taught the violence of close combat.

1084 marched to the training field, producing large clouds of dust from the dry grass intermixed with sand. The place reminded me of my small dusty practice football field of my youth. Those of us who have worn the gear can still feel the bone crunching impacts inflicted upon one another as young boys. Such places exist everywhere in the small towns of America. The thing about fields ingrained with pain is that even though we come and go from them; these places hold onto the pain that is shed upon them. The fields still hear my bells which rung in my head after the very hard hits.

I sensed the field and the many feelings of pain inflicted there throughout the decades of existence.

Dust rose up into my eyes and clogged my nose. However, I dared not wipe my nose on the march. I had been on the island for a bit of time now and knew better. The day was horribly hot as 1084 marched tightly at port arms. The dust collected upon the lenses of my BCGs and clouded my vision. But it's okay I didn't need to see in order to march.

On the island recruits must speak in the third person. Amongst my fellow recruits, I managed to hold onto threads of my personality, sneaking in conversations that are so important into the development of kinship between young men. However, during training, recruits were obligated to talk as warriors still in training in the third person, as we did not yet have the right to talk like Marines.

This recruit does not need to see, because this recruit hears the Drill Instructor sounding his marching cadence. He knows to keep his back straight and his elbows tucked. My masters have taught me to march in a straight line and this recruit must not disobey orders, and to do so would be sacrilege. He will walk straight into the jaws of battle unflinching, until told not to.

1084 arrived at the pugil stick arena. Any martial artist, be he a wrestler, boxer, MMA fighter, etc., can always feel and smell a ring. The scent is one intermixed with that sweet horrid mixture of nerves, fear, anxiety, anticipation, adrenaline, and bloodlust. I licked my teeth as I approached this modern day gladiatorial arena. I longed to give out some of the violence that was inflicted upon my body and my soul.

We circled up around the ring and the Close Combat Instructors strode before us. These Instructors were in the best place in the world to teach Martial Arts, each man and woman they teach will be a trained killer very soon. Each Marine possesses the abilities to rob an enemy of his life within 500 meters or less.

Although the violence experienced on the island cannot be measured, every action is completed according to a carefully designed risk model. My platoon was placed in a large circle around the ring and read a scripted but very important safety brief. The combatants in the ring wear a football helmet, mouth guard, neck roll, flak jacket (without ballistic plates) and a groin protector. The safety rules of when to stop the fight and illegal blows were also dictated to us.

A dreamer, even then I looked around my flanks and smiled

as I could both sense and feel the ongoing fear in the men around me. I went to boot camp the year after receiving my black belt in Karate. I loved fighting and licked my lips in anticipation for my upcoming bout.

A clean blow to the head from one of the previously trained techniques awarded points in these bouts. These techniques included a straight thrust, slash, horizontal butt stroke, vertical butt stroke, and a smash. The bouts were won by whoever could get three points first.

The recruits were organized according to body weight. I was around 165 lbs at the time and lined up with my mates. My stocky build made me look like I was 180 or so and intimated some of the other recruits near me. We sat in the timeless formation for all warriors to judge and learn from, the circle. The first two recruits were dressed for the combat. Not a man spoke and the air stung with anticipation for the action to begin.

The two men were checked by the CCIs outside the ring and then given permission to enter this circle of dark education. They were both young, perhaps no older than 18 each. However, they were no longer young boys. They both assumed their fighting stances, with their right legs back, and tensed their muscles like young lions prior to making their first kill. I felt it then as I do now whenever I watch combative contests. My hands turn cold, as I remind myself to lower my heart rate and to control my breathing.

The CCI blew his whistle and the fight began. The young warriors leapt at each other like abused pit bulls itching for a fight. They growled at one another and collided with the familiar crunch of the practice football field. However, here it was different. I could hear and sense the hatred fostered by the weeks of pain and training since on the island. The warriors unleashed hell upon one another in the way that they were trained. However, all violence ceased at the moment the Instructor blew his whistle.

This factor of leashed violence is one of the greatest tenets of Marine Corps discipline. In one moment, the mock bayonet battle looked as if two men were attempting to kill one another. They growled and tried to take each other's head off. Yet, all of this stopped in a tenth of second following the Instructor's whistle blast. This was a trained response. The recruits knew what would happen to them if they were dumb enough to ignore a command. They would have been quarter decked out there in the hot sun until they were unable to conduct another pushup.

This iron discipline is one portion of what makes the Marine Corps a favorite weapon within the arsenal of the United States military. Marines have the ability to conduct a wide variety of missions that require them to sling it out in the intense conditions in a pitched battle. At the same time, they can be expected to pull guard duty wearing dress blues at one of the nation's embassies or guard the President of the United States. Marines have the ability to turn violence on and off as one does a light switch. The problem comes when the Marine has done this too much, or is no longer under the iron control of Marine Corps.

The first point in the initial match was scored in under a second. The entire bout was decided in perhaps 15 seconds of combat. This early expose of battle was an excellent example of the swiftness of death on the field of battle. The difference of life and death in battle is measured in seconds and somehow always happens with a rising cloud of dust.

I was overly eager in waiting for my chance to take part in my own contest. The bouts continued and my turn was approaching. I watched as the other men in the flower of their youths continued to circle and collide with one another in the small pugil stick arenas. This was my coliseum for the time being and here I fought as a gladiator against other recruits. The bouts continued and the dust continued to rise.

PUGIL BOUTS

I was on deck and moved up to be dressed by my fellow recruits. Without access to boiling water, I used hot water from the sink taps of the head to mold my mouth guard. While it molded a little bit, it was still somewhat uncomfortable, producing a slight gag reflex that all contact athletes are familiar with.

I stepped into the groin protector, followed by my flak jacket. The armor fit snugly around my body. Next came the football helmet, whose piercing scent of soggy sweat brought back such lovely memories of my recent civilian youth. I put on the hockey gloves and was given my pugil stick.

As a martial artist, I felt at home in the ring. From watching the previous dozen bouts or so, I devised my plan. The recruits, as aggressive as they were, fought like amateurs. They charged head on into the fray as soon as the CCI blew the whistle. If they connected, it would prove devastating. But, like all experienced fighters, I knew how to employ angles during a one on one engagement. I decided to use them on my opponents. Additionally, I had previous training on the Bo staff from my days in the dojo. Even before I had the mock rifle in my hands, I knew what combinations I would use against my opponent before the opening whistle blast initiated the combat.

I waited there the in the stifling summer heat with the choking dust and the ill formed mouthpiece initiating the gag reflex in my throat. Waiting is a classic and stressful time that all warriors must experience. The anticipation of these moments seems to be amplified by the fact that you have to endure it with the extra pounds of body armor bearing down on you. My body heat increased and I tasted the salt dripping down from my nose into my mouth. I heard the other recruits panting now, as their match dragged on longer that either of them had probably anticipated. The DIs screamed at them to boil their blood, and to add energy to efforts in the fray...

I waited.

The scene of waiting has been played and replayed hundreds of times in the history of warfare. I felt as if I was a Greek hoplite burdened by the extra weight of his panoply, formed up in his phalanx waiting for his order to charge. The scene was perfect and historical battlefield romance added ambiance to this beautiful painting from the rising dust clouds created by the combative dances in these sawdust arenas. Heat, grunting, and dust serenaded me in this bloody expose. I closed my eyes, enjoying my final moments of rest prior to being unleashed upon my opponent. However, the noise of the combat was further enhanced when I closed my eyes. The air was filled with this horrible grog mixed with primordial screams, whistle blasts, and those indescribable crunching noises which is produced when men collide upon one another while wearing a full compliment of body armor.

A training dummy was set up outside the ring to practice striking techniques prior to a bout. I recalled my several combinations from my months spent with the Bo Staff. All fighters know that it is combinations that stand the best chance of breeching a defense. I was ready and determined to end my opponent.

A true warrior must learn to find peace in the chaos and the Marine Corps has patented this technique. This lesson came in handy to survive all my combat training throughout my military career as well as under the horrible drumbeats of the battlefield.

At war I am at peace
At peace in hell
Where my mother is pain
And my father is violence
And Death is my Mistress

Chaos is my bed
And sweat is my blanket
We learn to fear and to obey
We learn to become fear and make our enemies obey our will

We become masters of Death
As we become Death
We seek battle
We seek life
We seek to destroy

I am the Destroyer of men
I am fear
I am Nightmare

My eyes opened and I saw him. I saw my opponent waiting for me across the ring. He stirred from side to side, warming up his muscles outside the ring waiting in his on-deck position as I did. I could barely make out his eyes, obscured by dust and hidden by the shadows of his football helmet. I found my enemy.

Laying eyes on my opponent for the first time, whether while inside the training arena or on the field of battle was always a memorable moment. I thought at how fearsome this man looked standing erect in his body armor. He was short and powerfully built, just like me. My eyes were drawn to the tattoos drawn upon his tanned and powerfully appearing forearms. The tattoo on his forearm read "No Fear" and solidified my theory that this recruit, like most, would come charging straight toward me as soon as the whistle blast initiated the bout. I knew I had to check his initial charge and then he would be mine.

His gaze met mine and he hastily checked his nervous lateral stirring in an effort to appear more confident. I did the same and gave the same stare down that anyone who has ever participated in a contact sport is intimately familiar with. I looked at him and sought to dominate through my stare.

You are mine. I don't care what your name is or where you are from. Rather, I only desire one thing for you. I want to you lose. I want to hear you pant under my power and skill. I want you to beg for my mercy. I want to see defeat in your eyes, even before we first collide. You will be mine…

I will leave fear outside the ring. I leave hesitation and pain out here. I will only bring rage with me. I don't have hate in my heart, only power. You are mine.

It was my turn to enter the ring.

One of the Instructors gave me one final equipment safety check and then gave me the go ahead to enter the ring. My heart rate and breathing increased the moment I stepped into the ring and there was no fooling my body into relaxing. It would be the same as entering a house fire, telling yourself that everything is completely fine or expecting a wildebeest to relax as he crosses a river filled with crocodiles.

It is essential to remember that you are in fact an animal when one is in the business of war. Humans innately possess the wild instinct to kill if threatened. The only thing the military does is to make that wild killing instinct into an art form under the mask of control and a National Flag.

"Take a stance!" The CCI ordered to my opponent and me.

My opponent and I both stood there in our fighting stances and shouted: "Marine Corps!"

I stared into his eyes and he stared back into mine. We were held in this position for perhaps under two seconds, but the moment was another one of those places in time that will forever be burned into my warrior soul.

This recruit looks so much like me but I must destroy him. We wait for the signal.

The bout began with a whistle blast and the two of us were unleashed upon one another. He charged straight at me, just like I anticipated. I moved at an angle toward him, successfully dodging his blow and permitting me to land a horizontal butt stroke cleanly on the side of his helmet. My strike landed hard and stunned my opponent, nearly dropping him to the ground. Seeing my opponent weakened had the same effect that a lion would have seeing a gazelle splattered with blood from a swipe of his claws. My gaze was fixed upon him like a blood lusted predator.

"You're mine now, mother fucker." I quietly whispered under my breath.

Had I landed my blow in the heat of battle, the man's skull would have been cracked. The pain ensued by such a blow would have enabled me to kill him in seconds. The CCI reset us again in the middle of the ring with his command: "Take... a stance!" and our replies, "Marine Corps!" The bout continued and I beat my opponent with a resolute 3-0.

The day continued and the matches became ever more difficult as the recruits became more acclimatized to the body armor and to the ongoing bouts. I had three more matches that day and although they were closer than the first: I was undefeated in battle.

This day of pugil sticks was a welcomed entry into my mental journal of Parris Island training. The only momentary break from the supreme control of the Marines was when I was unleashed into the pure art form of battle or physical contests. These laborious breaks were by far my favorite portions of training on Parris Island.

Although a bit more free from the rigid constraints of training, each lesson was yet another element that made you into this paintbrush of chaos to be utilized at a later time on the canvas of war.

QUARTER DECKING

In battle, the room for error is minimal. The difference between life and death can at times hinge from something as small as moving one's muzzle a centimeter to one side prior to firing a round or jerking one's trigger instead of pulling it smoothly in the heat of a firefight. Warriors must have the self discipline to clean, check, and re-clean one's own gear. Failure to do so can mean death for a member of their unit. It means that another a child would have to grow up without his or her parent.

One would think a lesson with such grave circumstances could be easily learned by a mere lecture or a power-point slide. In theory that is a sound assessment. However, man is an animal whose greatest muse to cure inaction is pain. Men will act and strut with the prowess of a stallion for small periods of time. However, fatigue makes cowards of us all.

Pain is one of the Marine's greatest teaching assistants on the island and the quarterdeck is Pain's favorite lecture hall. The quarterdeck is the small area in between the DI hut and the head. It is here where a Marine recruit receives some of his most intensive physical training while on Parris Island. This fast becomes the necessary incentive to maintain a recruit's intensity level at epic rates.

A recruit was called to the quarterdeck for a number of reasons. The mistakes ranged from: an infraction during drill, an improperly polished belt buckle, or a perceived lack of discipline. When ordered to the quarterdeck, I immediately took off my cammie top and sprinted to this place of hell wearing only my tanned T-shirt, cammie trousers, and boots. Once a recruit stepped onto this small 20' x 20' area, he entered a hell within a hell.

It was typically the junior Green Belt Drill Instructors who were the lords in this small plain of torture. I sprinted up to them and formed a line with the other men who shared in my misfortune. I stood there at the position of attention and prepared myself.

My first time here, I reported with some men from my squad. My squad's drill was horrible. It began like every other training exercise on the island; with heart wrenching chaos and terror.

On the quarterdeck, the recruit is ordered to perform a number of calisthenics in rapid succession. It may not sound very different or more difficult than the rest of the training that one may do while on the island. However, this place can still bring back horrible memories; like my short amount of time spent on those yellow footprints.

It begins. "Side straddle hops! Go! Mountain climbers go! Pushups go! Run in place! Go! High knees! Faster Faster Faster! Leg lifts! Side Straddle Hops! Go! Flutter kicks! Go! Push ups! Go!"

When will this stop?? Fuck. I can't breathe but, he's not done with me yet. I know that when he commands I have to throw myself down faster than last time. I can't show weakness, he will only go harder. My lungs are on fire.

Within minutes my body was covered with sweat and my muscles were screaming for relief. The quarterdeck is this special little hot corner tucked away in this hell. While in it, I wanted to be out of it as quickly as I could. However, it seemed that the more I wished for rest, the less rest came. I stood there paralyzed in the small prison of pain, anger, and chaos. I stayed there and prayed for relief by trying harder. Regardless of how fit a recruit was, or thought they were, the quarterdeck was master. There was no beating it. Even as my fitness level improved, the Drill Instructors increased the level of intensity necessary to break a man. The quarterdeck is the perpetual mountain that never levels out. Rather, it continues to rise in elevation until the Drill Instructors assess a recruit was at the point to where a recruit was at their limit.

It is the sharpest of blades that require the hottest fires to mold them.

DISCIPLINE IS?

Marine Corps Drill Instructors dedicate every waking moment of a recruit's life on Parris Island to training. As my body was relentlessly sculpted by these sadistic Michelangelo's, my mind was tempered to survive the rigors of combat as well. While waiting in line for chow or a class to begin, the Drill Instructors constantly asked questions. This incessant drill made me able to learn definitions of different concepts and regulations verbatim.

"Sir, discipline is the instilling of willing obedience to orders, respect for authority, and teamwork, sir!"

The Marines found a perfect way to combine the atmosphere of chaos with deadly organized efficiency. They presented clear and concise orders to get recruits through this violence. Through this mechanism, Marines learn early on that if they follow orders they stand a chance of getting through any mess.

I learned early on in my military career that discipline is the cement that will keep men alive in battle. While on Parris Island, every order is given with the same intensity and fervor as if it was given to a platoon preparing to go reinforce a friendly platoon on a QRF mission (Quick Reaction Force).

It is years after this that I learned the importance of solid orders in the maelstrom of battle. Such teaching stayed with me in the years of peacetime military life. They saved lives when I practiced their lessons in my graduate school of war: the Pech River Valley, Kunar Province, Afghanistan. Yet, that is another tale to be told.

ON INFANTRY OPERATIONS: MOVING TO THE FIGHT

"Every Marine is a rifleman." This statement was continually pumped into my head before and during my time at Parris Island. The idea of becoming riflemen or even an infantryman sounds extremely exciting. Young men have always been long drawn to starring in these roles of shirtless heroes who walk with rippling muscles and carry large machine guns. These fictional heroes carry hundreds of rounds tightly slung round their tanned bodies. They appear to sprint the entire time on the battlefield and through each phase of their fictional missions. They simply seem to stride on the battlefield as if they were instead performing figure skating.

To the untrained eye, it is easy to see why so many young men would aspire to become legends such as Rambo or commando. It is difficult not to be impressed by these statuesque warrior heroes. However, those who have been in the infantry or conducted infantry training know better. It is only after training and later experiencing combat that we come to find that these characters who inspire us are in fact missing a vital element to combat: weight.

In the vast majority of movies that portray combat; the main focus of the depiction is during the final phase: the attack. The main majority of the populous will only see the armies arrayed in their neat and ordered formation, ready for the upcoming fight. Even in modern day, the online observers to the hundreds of videos displaying battlefields in Afghanistan will bear witness to the final intense moments where contact erupts.

Warriors, and especially infantrymen, all long for that moment of contact with the mysterious enemy. However, there is a vital problem in finding what we seek... we have to close with the enemy first. On any movement to contact, warriors do not move as stealthy muscled panthers. We do not move gracefully, like ninjas, as one might expect after watching 007 or more recently Jason Bourne. Instead, we are something much more grotesque in appearance. Warriors instead move like they are pack mules. The nickname "Marius's Mules" was a fitting name to the Roman legionnaires who first began carrying a heavy kit, in order to reduce the large Roman *impedimentus* or baggage train. Anyone, who has carried a weapon and a pack on a forced march can tell you his or her past horrors. It is a physical experience like the rest of Parris Island that is difficult to give justice through by mere words.

FIRST HUMP (HIKE)

I caught wind of the first humps approach. In laymen terms, a hump meant walking fast with a 35 lb ALICE pack (ruck sack) and a rifle. I ran cross-country in high school for the couple of years prior to arriving to Parris Island. Naturally, when I heard we were going to be walking for five miles, I initially scoffed at it. I mean, how hard could walking a few miles at a brisk pace actually be?

PACKING LIST

Control remained a constant presence, even in regard to the packing list. SSgt Insco and Sgt Staley provided instruction on how to carefully pack the items into our ALICE packs. First, I placed the wet weather bag inside the ALICE pack. The wet weather bag is essentially a large green waterproof bag about the size of a small garbage bag. I initially was unclear as to what was the point of this thing. After all, could dry clothes really make that much difference when you are being shot at? If you're a combat veteran or an experienced hiker you have probably learned the huge difference that dry socks can make on one's morale and even ability to survive.

Piece by piece the DIs went over the necessary items to be packed, in the amount of detail that cocaine smugglers take in crossing the U.S. border. Each shirt, sock, skivvy, and uniform was folded as tightly as they possibly could. These carefully folded articles of clothing were then jam packed into zip lock bags. I ensured that they were airtight by slowly closing the bags, pausing to suck the air out, and finally sealing the zip lock bag.

Platoon 1084 carefully packed in the fashion ordered by the Drill Instructors. Everything had its place. This is done in the event you are wounded or killed that every Marine in the platoon immediately knows where to get a prescribed piece of gear.

Space within one's pack is critically important during dismounted operations. As a recruit, I though it was more of the Marine's mentality for being hard asses and to express attention to detail. However, after experiencing combat for myself, I finally found out why space was so much more important. A warrior needs extra space for more important things like water and ammunition.

I prepared my kevlar helmet for the hike. It was my first time wearing it and I was horribly excited to do so. I used a small portion of my precious free time to ensure that my helmet fit properly and comfortably on my head. I took my time ensuring the sweatband was molded to comfortably fit upon my head. We who are warriors know that one must do whatever it takes to preserve what little comfort is possible during a forced march.

Wearing the kevlar, I walked to the dreaded quarter deck area. It was free time still, and the DI's lowered their prowling patrols amongst us and for the most part remained in the DI hut. There was also a mirror placed on the quarterdeck. I intermittently catch glimpses of my face as it became more and more chiseled throughout the training. I walked to it, wearing the kevlar and gazed at my face in the mirror.

I thought to myself: "Wow, I actually look like Marine dressed for combat."

I have always found mirrors to be a peculiar object. It is one of the few items on earth that permit one to stare directly back into the windows of your soul. I stared at myself and even though I had only been at the island for perhaps two weeks, I looked unfamiliar. I gazed into my dark eyes for perhaps only a few seconds. However, this stare has survived for over a decade. It lives now within me and in my heart. At that moment, I stared directly into the windows of my warrior soul still developing in that womb called Parris Island.

WOMB

At Parris Island a recruit is a warrior fetus, developing for a life dedicated to war. I grew in the womb of this bitch that is the Island. As I developed, I heard the lullabies sung by my makers. However, they are not the sweet songs of twinkle, twinkle, or rock-a-bye baby. Rather, these melodies are of the cacophonic songs of war and battle. These screams of orders and gung-ho replies are the songs preparing one for the world he is shortly to be born into. I developed for a world adorned with the greatest atrocities of mankind: War.

A Marine is not born as a helpless baby. Rather, a Marine is tossed out of the womb ready for the plains of war. The warrior will possess the ability to hike for miles in search of the enemy. Once you lay your eyes upon him, you will have the ability to tear him into shreds and drink of his blood.

STEP OFF

1084 was awakened, fed, and watered. My Platoon hastily returned to the barracks and suited up for the upcoming hike. I put on my deuce gear composed of my green cartridge belt, canteens, magazine pouches, butt pack, and suspenders. My canteens were full since last night, but I wanted to be sure, as I knew the heat would not forgive any man unlucky enough to not have water. I opened the canteens and was relieved to see them still topped off. I buttoned my cartridge belt and then picked up my rucksack.

I lifted this burden over my head and dropped it so that it fell upon my shoulders. I was being introduced to that common enemy that all combat veterans are intimately familiar with: weight. I grabbed my rifle, slung it over my shoulder, and moved outside to join the rest of my mates.

C Company formed up behind the barracks as the sky was blowing us a kiss with the cooling breeze of dawn. The morning report was given to the Company First Sergeant.

The command: "Right Face!" was given. "Forward... March.... Route step... march."

"Here we go." I thought to myself.

The pace was not terribly difficult as we moved through the garrison portion of Parris Island. This slow pace was not for leisure; rather it was for a reason. The Marines move slowly at first in order to assess how the equipment felt on their bodies. After a few minutes, my platoon conducted a quick halt to do a gear check.

This two-minute gear check was a very important portion of this and any hike. It allows the individual to adjust any gear that might not be feeling just right on the body. Sometimes something as little as pulling a wrinkle out of a sock can prevent a horrible blister to form, allowing an individual to move faster and fight harder under the burden of contact.

1084 was on the move again. Marine recruit formations are arranged by height, with exception of the squad leader. The squads were roughly composed of twenty-five a piece. These large squads were more of an administrative body and column, not necessarily for tactical considerations. The tallest recruits were set to the front and the shortest ones, like me standing at 5' 6", were at the "little end" of the formation.

Anyone that has conducted a formation ruck march or run will tell you about the horrors inflicted by the enemy who is created by merely moving, commonly referred to as "the slinky effect." This evil term has also been deemed as the "accordion effect" by some in the military. This horrible occurrence is a result of the entire formation attempting to keep the swift pace with the very lead elements. What inevitably happens is that at times the rear of the formation is hiking at nearly five miles per hour.

The Marines hate the slinky effect and have engendered several clever orders to counter that from occurring. The order "tighten up" was echoed continually by the DIs on the march. In horribly tied unison, the recruits all shouted with the breath they have to spare.

"Tighten up! The DIs ordered.

"Aye Sir!" We ferociously replied.

The pace was violent and I extended my stride to keep up with the recruit in front of me.

Nothing is easy about a Marine Corps hump. I have run six marathons and I think that I have been tested more in any Marine hump I have been on. These are the furthest things possible from a leisurely Sunday nature hike that I can think of.

I felt like an overworked horse pulling a wagon at an unrealistic pace. The thing is the Marines made this extremely difficult pace possible to maintain. Iron discipline was law during the march. If the platoon failed to sound off, we were ordered to respond with longer and longer answers to the questions asked by the DIs. The DIs asked questions for a few desired results. This constant repetition of Q's and A's ensured memorization.

Most of all it reinforced the recruits' ability to respond under the yoke of the fatigue laced chaos. Anyone can be intense to lift a few hundred pounds on bench press or sprint a few hundred meters. However, the ability to stay calm and make well educated decisions in dire situations is what permits professional warriors to destroy the enemy as well as keep the men charged under one's supervision alive and unharmed.

Slowly, I learned to accept the pain, fear, and exhaustion. I started to become immune to this sick regimen. I was able to feel fear, but say fuck it. The Marines were making my fellow recruits and me into finely tuned instruments for war.

1084 hiked into the woodlands of Parris Island and strode as miniature grim reapers in the shadows of these majestic trees. This land was much different from my familiar woodlands composed of deciduous trees in Michigan. I was at peace here during the march. My cardio vascular fitness was at very high levels and I was able to mitigate some of the effects of the march.

"Is this what the forests in Virginia looks like?" I snuck the question to Recruit Haynes who was next to me on the march.

My feet began to burn. It was my first time feeling this sensation and I had no idea what this was about. As intense as the regimen of Parris Island was, it is done smartly, efficiently and most of all safely. We took a halt shortly after the three-mile mark. The purpose of this halt was not so we could take a breath and wipe away our sweat. Rather, the recruits were weapons that needed maintenance.

I took my boots and socks off, like the rest of the recruits near me. I saw them: my first blisters. My feet were unaccustomed to both wearing military style boots as well as hiking. The blisters at this stage were little more than hot spots. Their effects were mitigated through the healthy application of foot powder and moleskin. Following my feet; I tended to my rifle. I broke it down "shotgun style" allowing the upper receiver to hang freely, thus exposing the bolt. I reassembled the weapon after placing a light coat of CLP on the bolt.

We were soon on the march back toward garrison. We continued the hump, or as what the DIs called a little "nature walk" because of the mere five-mile distance we were traversing on the island. We moved under the weight of the ALICE packs under the horrible echoes of memorable phrases such as "Tighten up! General orders! First SgtMAJ of the Marine Corps… and birthplace of the Marine Corps??!"

1084 returned to the barracks and back into the hearth of the chaos. At least I was happy to get that godforsaken pack off my shoulders.

Humps in the Marine Corps is one the celebrated past times of all Marines. They are always tough and grueling. Marines take these hard-learned lessons with them into the fleet and into their lives. Many can hump for miles with loads exceeding 80 lbs, even long after they have traded their six pack abs for a gut.

DRINK WATER!

It is said that an Army marches on its stomach. I do not refute this fact. However, a human can go days into weeks without food. Although, not having adequate food is completely miserable, you won't die. Dehydration can occur much quicker. An average person will die after not having water for three days. Dehydration can occur within hours while conducting strenuous military operations, regardless of the temperature.

If there is one thing that the Marines do well at Parris Island; it is ensuring that you do not succumb to heat exhaustion. A canteen, like my rifle, was always with me or staged within a couple hundred meters. Drill Instructors conducted their PT runs and humps by carrying a two-quart canteen strapped to their upper backs.

I constantly drank water. Drinking water becomes religious,

and the Marines gave this sacrament several times a day. Throughout my time on the island, the Marines practice forced hydration. This may sound cruel, but like everything else on the island it is done for a reason: to save life both in training and at war. Many mornings began by holding a full canteen and drinking its entire contents within a few minutes, culminating by showing proof by holding the empty canteen over one's head.

I never paid attention to the color of my urine prior to my time at Parris Island. Color coded charts were displayed in every classroom, head, and training facility at Parris Island. The darker the urine, the more dehydrated a person was. The goal was to try to have one's urine as clear as possible.

Fear was another motivational aspect utilized to ensure Marine recruits continually drink water throughout their training. I was told the standard operating procedure that the Navy Corpsmen would perform on us, should a recruit go down as a heat casualty. The corpsmen had to attain the Recruit's core temperature as soon as possible. For this crucial time where life hung in the balance, the beloved Navy docs had a specialized tool: the silver bullet.

The silver bullet was an anal thermometer which read the heat casualty's core temperature. 1084 was warned, that unless a recruit wanted to experience this thermometer being shoved into their rear ends; they should always drink water. It was a very effective technique, to say the very least.

CLASSES

Classroom time in the Marine Corps was a break of sorts, in that I was not panting or marching in the searing heat of the summer sun. However, the Marine Corps perfected their art of hardening warriors down to a science. These classrooms were a far cry from the lovely university lectures that I would come to love as a graduate student. Rather, on Parris island I sat in classrooms at the position of attention, with my heels together, back straight, and hands either on a book or pen, or with fingers joined on my thighs. This environment possessed a challenge of its own: staying awake.

These classrooms by Parris Island standards were very comfortable. The air-conditioning kept the temperature at roughly 72 degrees. This was in sharp contrast to the nearly 95 degree heat outside. The environment was ideally suited for a nap. This was a hazard for recruits.

Military training feeds off intensity and excitement. The classroom was a 180 from the rest of the training curriculum. Any Marine or Soldier can tell you about the great difficulty that is involved in attempting to stay awake in a classroom, where lessons, while very important, are extremely mundane.

The Drill Instructors patrolled the rows of desks in search of weary recruits. I was always a good student and it was strange to have that feeling of drowsiness within the classroom. All Marines intimately know the signs of fatigue all too well. One's head begins to bob up and down as you fall on the verge of unconsciousness. I never fell asleep. I had enough sense to stand up and move to the back of the large lecture hall the moment that fatigue set in.

LINE TRAINING

The tenets of shock and ferocity were ever present on the training grounds of Parris Island. They were especially present while we learned the art of close combat. Marines love learning new ways to slaughter their enemy on the field of battle. In the last decade of the twentieth century, the Marine Corps taught the martial art system known as LINE: Linear Infighting, Neural, Override system. The infamous MCMAP system came about during the birth of the 21st century.

I came to Parris Island with my Black Belt in Karate. It felt comfortable standing in a fighting stance learning the techniques of this brutal system. The system involved a highly-synchronized technique platform which emphasized speed, joint manipulation, pain delivering techniques which culminated in killing blows.

I enjoyed this system and loved the sheer simplistic brutality of it. Many of the techniques I was privy to learn ended by taking an opponent to the ground and finishing them with a killing blow. A stomp to the head for example was very appropriate.

The CCIs would ask us: "How high?"

We answered: "Head high, sir!" as we lifted our right legs up, gained momentum, and simulated a life ending stomp to our opponent's head.

USMC HISTORY

The Marine Corps is the only branch of service where the history of its branch is taught in its initial training. Marines pride themselves in this aspect and its utter importance. The Marine Corps is the smallest of the uniformed services, next to the Coast Guard. Every Marine whether new to the fleet or well advanced in age can flawlessly recite the facts covering the Marine Corps illustrious history.

The Marine Corps birthday and its birthplace are amongst the holiest tenets of the Marine Corps culture. These teachings are forever ingrained in Marines and never leave them. The site of Tunn Tavern, Philadelphia and the date of November 10th, 1775 are as sacred as the date of Christmas to most people.

Marines pride themselves in learning this heroic history, which they must maintain through their own valorous acts on the field of battle. I was taught to respect the past wars and battles that the Marines originated from. The common factor that Marines are taught is that they are simply better both on and off the battlefield than every other branch of service in the United States Military.

Marines cannot fail in battle and will win at any costs. The Marines are to be feared by civilians and/or enemies alike. The very nickname "Devil Dog" was a gift from German opponents in World War I. During the battle of Belleau Wood, the Germans called Marines "Tuefel Hunden" for their ferocity in combat. In the Korean War, I was reminded that while the Army abandoned thousands of pieces of equipment during the retrograde of the Chosin Reservoir, the Marines made a fighting retreat with all their equipment and men.

The history of the Marine Corps is stained upon any man or women who has earned the title. It never leaves them.

BARRACKS

1st Recruit Training Battalion, Charlie Company, sits on the Northern border of Parris Island. It lies on the edge of the infamous marshlands which separated Parris Island from South Carolina proper. The location of these barracks almost seemed too fitting for this Warrior womb.

My platoon held formations to the rear of the barracks facing these fiercely dark and imposing marshlands. I stood there in the mornings locked at parade rest while my Drill Instructors saluted with their morning reports.

I learned to find peace when I could on the island. The peace came intermittingly, as I found it did later in battle. I embraced these small glimpses of calm when the commands of my masters did not tear sky round my ears. One has too to remain sane.

"Right Face!" My company was marched to the large PT field just to the north of 1st Recruit Training Battalion. I held my canteen with my elbow bent at 90 degrees and marched smartly to the PT field. I was wearing my Tan T-Shirt, green shorts, BCGs, and of course my go fasters.

1084 marshaled on the PT field in celebration of the warrior spirit to exercise our bodies. Each PT session was started with the "Marine Corps daily dozen." This was a mixture of stretching and calisthenics designed to warm you up for physical training of the day. Each exercise had a different and confusing name for different exercises. They ranged from "side- straddled hops, cherry pickers, hello dollies, and the beloved Marine Corps push ups."

The recruits conducted the physical training with the same intensity and gusto like always. The physical training plans followed a well-planned regimen consisting of circuit training, distance runs, ability group runs, and circuit training. PT was in fact challenging, however the transformation of a recruit during his time on the island is not merely as a result of these hour-long PT sessions. The entire experience of Recruit training is a physical test. A body becomes hardened not only from the humps or quarterdecking. Rather a recruit is always holding a pose to stand or sit erect. During my waking hours I was holding one of the several yoga-like poses as directed in the manual of arms. Slowly, I began to embody and look like the warrior I was supposed to become.

OBSTACLE COURSE

I considered myself to be a very strong young man. I could bench press nearly 300 lbs, although I only weighed around 160 lbs or so. My body was well tailored to fighting from years of martial arts, weight lifting, football, wrestling, and cross country. I was strong. However, as I came to find, combat conditioning is something completely different than what I would have came to expect.

To be fit for war does not necessarily mean you can curl 55 pounds per arm or run six miles in under an hour. A fighting man must maintain agility and the will to continue to fight on limited hours of sleep or food. As the training progressed that summer, I was further educated into what it took to get a warrior fit for combat.

I was only on Parris Island for roughly three weeks and my body was changing. I was becoming ever leaner and more agile than I have ever been in my life. Soon it was my turn to be physically challenged even more. It was time to have a go on the obstacle course.

My mates and I were marshaled one early morning to the rear of the company. I wore the uniform composed of my tan T-shirt, cammie trousers, boots, and of course canteens. 1084 marched to the cadence sung by the DIs confidently in a slow solid march.

The command double-time sounded and 1084 made the short jog to the infamous "O" Course.

I was then and am still not a large fan of heights. I knew that a good portion of the obstacle course would be spent 8-20 feet off the ground. I was less than thrilled to partake of this training exercise. 1084 halted near this strange collection of metal bars, logs, and ropes. A left face was ordered and my platoon awaited the safety brief and demonstration.

A very lean and powerful looking Drill Instructor came before the recruits. He gracefully breezed through each obstacle as if he were merely taking a leisurely jog on a Saturday morning. This man, like all Drill Instructors, was the epitome of what the Marines considered to be warriors. I nervously watched this man as he effortlessly made it over each set of bars, ropes, and logs. My hands beaded with sweat in nervous anticipation. Soon, it was my turn.

The recruits assembled into squads and faced the beginning of the obstacle course. The entrance to the obstacle course was marked by a small three-foot log followed by a large steel horizontal bar. The Drill Instructors controlled the chaos by ordering my mates when to charge. I moved closer and closer to the beginning of my squad. These small beads of sweat made my hands slick to the touch and my stomach swelled in small nervous loops. There was no stopping it; I was up.

The DI gave the signal to commence my charge. The first small log was just something to help activate my heart rate and get my system going for the upcoming battle. I ran to the parallel bar and began my attack. The more agile recruits could perform the technique called "the college boy roll." This movement propelled the recruit up and over the bars, in the same manner that a gymnast might do. I was not capable of performing that technique, but luckily my upper body strength was usually enough to compensate for my lack of agility. I pulled myself over the bar, to where I could hang my armpit over the bar or what the Marines called: "chicken winging it." With the successful chicken wing on the bar, I was able to kick up into the air, generating enough momentum to propel myself over.

I bounded over a couple more logs and met my next major obstacle. I jumped up to another large parallel bar and slid down bars which angled down at 45 degrees for about five meters or so. Once successfully negotiated, I moved to another large log and walked down the slope of a 45-degree sloping beam.

I pressed on and at this point in the course, my heart rate was increasing, and my muscles began to burn. A large log, perhaps around six feet high, stood before me. I jumped up and scrambled over this obstacle, grabbing the sawdust as I bounded up and over it. I advanced, under the screams of other recruits and the Drill Instructors. I became lost in the sheer energy and intensity of the moment. It is only after fighting in combat does one realize the sheer genius of the Marine Corps training model at Parris Island. The Marines truly have found a method to replicate the intensity of battle, before the first round ever graces a recruit's ears.

My mates and I continued to push ourselves as if we were slashing through the rear area of the enemy's defenses. I bounded over a few more small logs and hit the wall. Here, I again utilized the handy climbing technique of chicken winging to negotiate the wall. I moved over the wall and bounded over a few more sets of logs. I finagled my body over the double sets of parallel bars and moved toward the rope climb.

I took hold of the rope and began pulling. My muscles were on fire and I could not perfect the technique of "biting" the rope in between my legs. However, I pressed on, going hand over hand.

About halfway up the rope, I had nothing left. Without utilizing my legs, I would not be able to perform this climb.

I climbed down in defeat. I was a failure and felt the sinking feeling of utter defeat in my stomach. Maybe I didn't have what it took to be a Marine after all. I thought to myself how embarrassing it would be to return home without the title of Marine. For an instant, hope was fleeting from my soul.

Much to my surprise my Senior Drill Instructor did not chastise me. He asked: "Did you make it up the rope recruit?"

"Sir, no Sir!" I answered.

"Why not?!"

"No excuse, sir!"

"Well, looks like you'll just have to next time."

"Sir, yes, sir!"

"Get out of my face, recruit!"

As brutal as the movies and stories about Parris Island may in fact be, there is a portion in this training model rarely spoken of. The DIs want recruits to be the best Marines they can be on graduation day. Although, SSgt Telford did not ask me if was okay or sad, his eyes betrayed him. He had calming gray eyes, whose color reminded me of a majestic mountain. He was a strong and aggressive warrior. However, I knew he cared about me.

This Marine brotherhood can be seen in the eyes of those training us for this horribly difficult profession of war. These Drill Instructors for the most part were not old men, broken down. Rather, they were in the prime of their careers. They were young men, some only in their mid twenties. They remembered what it was like for them during their own time on the island.

I was determined to climb the rope the next time I encountered it. In my barracks, we had a pull up bar and a hanging rope for use during free time. I spent the next several nights perfecting the bite with my feet. I nailed it in about two days. The next time I encountered the rope, I would conquer it.

CHAPEL

One of the sad truths is that as warriors grow older they may only become spiritual during times of great need. This can occur at war or when warriors undergo a particular hardship. Perhaps this is why the bible chooses the desert as the setting for so many of its heroes to find themselves. Parris island is the perfect setting for warriors to discover peace through spirituality. It is when we see death that we also see God.

Sundays are a sacred time on the island, as there are no major training events. However, the training does not cease and it is a day reserved for uniform inspection prep, weapon maintenance, quarterdecking, drill, and most importantly the chapel.

Recruits are given the choice to attend worship service for a religion of their choice. As a decent enough Catholic, I chose to attend mass on Sundays as well as serve as the platoon's lay reader, saying the nightly prayers for the platoon. On Parris Island, I believe I attended some of the most influential services in my entire life.

The mere act of going to church was a gift of freedom. It was one of the few times that recruits were permitted to walk unescorted without a Drill Instructor. There were about 15 practicing Catholics in my platoon. I loved marching with them, unbothered by the sadistic-seeming Drill Instructors. It was like a breath of fresh air to be on our own on this short perhaps five- minute walk to the recruit chapel. I smiled, as it was one of few times where I could relax and actually take account of what in God's name I was doing with my life.

We stepped into the church and the first thing that struck my ears and eyes was not a religious matter whatsoever. I saw girls.

On Parris Island, male and female Marine recruits are kept segregated from one another. I saw or heard them from time to time. Occasionally, I heard the female Drill Instructors calling cadence. Their voices shined like emeralds in the darkness of this place. Males are forbidden to interact with the females during mass. However, their mere presence seemed to remind me of the world long forgotten of my youth.

Something occurred to me nearly at each and every mass, I cried. As I listened to the songs or the sermon being told by the priest, I truly felt the sadness of what I was doing there. I thought of being away from my family and my girlfriend. Life was difficult at Parris Island and I truly asked God to help me several times a day.

Crying during Mass was not an occurrence unique to me. Many of the proud warriors near me did the same. Here in the chapel, under the protection of God, I allowed warrior guard to be at ease and admitted to myself what I really was, I was nothing but a young boy. Here, under the light cascading from the chapels stain glass windows I realized what I was training for. Like many of my mates, I was one of those lost souls who sought something beyond merely going to college, finding a decent job, and buying a house. I sought to explore those dark uncharted areas of life and of the human experience.

I sought the darkness and trained for this horrible phenomenon in human affairs known as war. Everything I did on the Island had but one sole purpose: so that one day I might meet the enemy and turn him into a pile of minced muscle and bone.

I drank heavily of the wines called fear and chaos on the island. I moved as a drunk man in a bar during my war exercises. Chaos was my world and my only relief came when I finally closed my eyes when I was granted sleep.

Here in the Chapel, I was sheltered from that world of horrid yelling and violence. For a mere 60 minutes I was not a student of killing. Rather, I was able to drink of something much stronger. I enjoyed the sweet wine of hope and love.. For many recruits, Parris Island was the most traumatic experience they had gone through. For myself, it in fact was at that point in my young life.

I savored every moment of the mass. During communion I was saddened by the fact that the Mass was almost over and I soon had to return back to my Drill Instructors.

With the mass concluded, I walked outside with my platoon mates. For a few minutes, I felt indestructible and the actions of my Drill Instructors could not phase me. Perhaps, I was correct in this theory. However, fatigue and the punishment of pain inflicted en masse could break even the most hardened believers.

FIRE WATCH MEDITATIONS... I DO THIS FOR YOU

The entire platoon was on a roster for the 60-minute fire watch (night guard) requirement. It came down to each man having it perhaps once a week. A recruit's main duties for fire watch was to ensure that no recruit left the barracks, keep order, and do the platoon's laundry.

Although I lost an hour of sleep, I thoroughly enjoyed this time. It was a peaceful mediation for me where I could think on my own and not be bothered by the hardships of my masters. I wore my cammies, boots, a cover, deuce gear, and a red lens flashlight. I patrolled the entire length of the squad bay and the head with another recruit. I would not talk to the other recruit except for when we initially started the shift. Even if I could talk to him, I doubt I would have.

I loved listening to the sound of my boots slowly walking up and down the hallway of the squad bay in my barracks. However, there was a downside to thinking a lot. Especially when a young man contemplates the consequences of his actions. If you are not careful, you may actually realize what the hell you are doing. You may experience a moment of clarity.

There is one night I remember distinctly. I walked the lonely squad bay with my red lens flashlight, contemplating my destiny. I missed my girlfriend and my family. I was uncertain if I had made the right decision for my life. There, walking the beat on fireguard, I let my mental guard down. I was not this iron recruit standing tall and erect. I was not pretending to be a brave warrior who was ready to drink of the enemy's blood upon first contact. I was not pretending to be cocky or fearless.

Rather, at that moment I became what I really was. I was a kid who had just turned 18 a few months ago that had signed nearly a half-decade of his life away to serve under the flag of the United States of America. I was honestly scared out of my fucking mind. Was this worth it? I was not a man, yet but I was most certainly about to join the profession of hunting the most dangerous game.

I was not going to cry. However, I felt a large lump in my throat pull me deeper and deeper into the depths of sadness and uncertainty. I asked God if I was doing the right thing and to give me strength in the upcoming days, weeks, and months ahead. Above everything else, all I wanted was to become a United

States Marine. I was uncertain if I had the strength to successfully undertake this immense challenge.

With tears welling up in my eyes and my stomach in knots, I paused to stare out of the window to find solace. I was hoping that perhaps somewhere in the dark shadows I would find a glimmer of Pandora's dew called hope. It was then when I found exactly what I was looking for.

I stared out and caught sight of one of the most beautiful and memorable scenes in my entire life. The American flag was brilliantly illumined by the streetlights, as the crowning piece to the Iwo Jima memorial across the parade deck. She danced brilliantly to the tune of the fresh summer night's breeze. She danced just for me in that moment; the exact way I needed her to.

My mouth drew open as I breathlessly watched my flag. Although she was perhaps 400 meters away from me, I swore I heard her. I heard the distinctive flapping that only a flag makes in the wind. She filled my heart with the hope I was looking for. Chills flowed down my spine throughout the entire length of my body as if the waters from Niagara Falls cascaded upon me in the chill of winter.

I looked at her with tears rolling down my cheeks and without commanding or thinking of it; a sentence was spoken from my mouth.

"I do this for you."

I felt like a love-struck boy finally making eye contact with the woman he loved. Warriors join up and are motivated to serve for different reasons. I had many, but I think the most important aspect within my collage of inspiration is that I believe my country is worth defending at any cost, even my body.

I do this for you.

Iwo Jima Memorial at Parris Island

SWIM TEST

Every Marine is a rifleman; a rifleman that is excepted to bring shock and death from the sea. The very etymology of the word Marine derives from the Latin *Mare*, sea. The tradition of bringing death from the sea stems back from the Marines of the American Revolutionary times, where precise rifle fire was necessary to clear the enemy off nearby ships.

Swim week was a small break from the hot South Carolina Sun. I spent at least half the day there throughout the week in the large training pool. I was a decent swimmer, meaning that I would not drown and could perform a half ass free style stroke to cover some distance. This portion of the training did not cause a great deal of anxiety to me. However, one could still sense the anxiety from some of the unskilled or non-swimmers. Some of the young recruits were even frightened by the idea of getting into the water.

The first trial was simply to see who was able to swim the 25 meters across the pool. I had no problem conducting this small task. However, some of the recruits did and were brought to the side for personal instruction.

It was very strange to watch existence of care and compassion exuded by many of the Marine Instructors on Parris Island. Throughout my military career, I have found that the best leaders behave as wolves. They might be ready to show their fangs and slash open flesh at a moment's notice. At the same time, they must be ready to lick and nurture a struggling cub. I watched some of the remedial training that went on and I was impressed by the level of attention and passion in the voices of the Instructors.

The weak swimmers looked horribly frightened. A few solitary tears dripped down some of the recruit's faces. They did not want to go further into the deeper end. This was another stunning example where calm and confident leadership can make men willing to go further into the depths of their greatest fears. Men are willing to walk through the dark gates of hell as long as you illuminate the way with the light called confident leadership.

Training continued and I learned the various techniques to survive in a war environment. I continued to tread water and make various flotation devices with my uniform. I found this week to be quite pleasant as compared to the rest of boot camp. After the training day was complete, we were sent to the locker room to change out of wet cammies. This simple act became a luxury to me—changing that is. I was able to do something without the total control of my masters wearing the fear enhancing campaign covers. Changing into dry clothes here without the expected countdown made me feel quite normal. One learned to revel in the few moments where yells did not tear the sky about your ears.

One also learned to appreciate the subtle beauty of women in those few breaths we could look upon one of them. For the most part, male recruits are not permitted any contact with women throughout training. Swim week permitted one such exception. The Marine Combat Swim Instructors were all stunning physical specimens. The thing was that one of these Instructors just happened to be a gorgeous blonde.

The Instructors wore tan T-shirts and UDTs. These form-fitting shorts are designed for a purpose and to ensure a swimmer receives minimal drag through the water. The other unintended consequence of these shorts is that they leave very little to the imagination. After not seeing the female form in this much detail for over a month it was difficult not to gawk over this woman.

Her beautiful body reminded me of many things. She reminded me that I was but a young man, in the budding of my life as both a warrior and as a man. Her breasts reminded me of those late nights spent with girls back home. She reminded all of the sweet taste of that highly coveted wine of freedom I desperately wished for. This sergeant moved so nimbly and gracefully. She moved like a puma amongst us bloodthirsty wolves.

The DIs knew what was on the minds of all the recruits. It was plain to see that each recruit was having the vivid fantasies that all young men have. Later that night, the DIs promised that the platoon would be quarter decked for hours on end if he caught any of the recruits disrespecting this gorgeous non-commissioned officer with our eyes. This threat and order worked and prevented us from outright leering at this woman.

Swim training increased in both complexity and intensity. I

learned the importance of sealing the waterproof bag in my AL-ICE pack. It was not only done to ensure that a Marine had dry clothes in battle. Rather, it was to ensure that the packs could be used as a floatation device.

I continued to jump and swim in my full combat gear. It was awkward learning to swim on your back with a full pack, kevlar, and a rifle. Inevitably, I choked on water a good deal, but the training helped me fend off the urge to panic and dumping my gear. I was becoming ever more disciplined and learned more about the warrior craft.

1084 was tested on individual abilities in swimming on the final day of swim week. I was happy with having it done and was sent to the locker room as soon I finished testing. I thoroughly enjoyed changing on my own again. My small furlough of freedom was extended for a few moments more as the recruits moved back in small teams to Charlie Company. I moved closer toward the end of the boot camp tunnel.

CONFIDENCE COURSE

Knowing fear and learning to overcome it is one of the best skills a warrior can acquire in training. For those of us that have tasted combat, we know that we do not enter the shadow of battle with enthusiasm or set to catchy background music. Rather, the truth is even though warriors may lust for a contact to begin, they start the action with dread brewing in the depths of their souls. It is a truth that many in the profession of arms rarely admit.

No matter who you were in this horrible place, Parris Island found a way to trigger fear. Whether it was fear of heights, suffocation from CS gas, water, heat exhaustion, physical fitness, shooting, to taking a shit of front of someone, or the unknown. This fear was not dealt in a slow manner.

Fear was not sampled in the manner one might sample wine. Rather, fear was served on a sampling platter of full shots of horrible whiskey. I slammed these shots one after the other and under the direct supervision of the Drill Instructors. This fear entered my system and hit my blood within seconds. The Marines teach to taste and quickly swallow fear. Marines feel fear, but say fuck it.

For me, heights became this monster called fear. To this day, I still hate heights. The idea of falling and dying was not what frightened me the most; it was falling and living. However, the fear of not becoming a United States Marine frightened me even more. I said fuck it and moved over each of these horrible obstacles.

Visions of Recruit Lawrence or Gomer Pile from the legendary Marine movie *Full Metal Jacket* played through my head on the day of that event. Gomer Pile represented weakness. Weakness in Parris Island was not tolerated. In battle, weakness or the inability to keep up with one's platoon mates can cost mission hit time and perhaps more tragically can get a Marine killed. I did not permit my fear to keep me from completing the task at hand.

Whether it is on the battlefield or on the horrid training grounds of the American South, warriors learn to meet and deal with fear. We all have our own ways of dealing with it. I chose to swallow mine. I swallowed this horrible liquid with a reluctant gulp. I took her all in and proceeded with my task at hand.

Each obstacle challenged a Marine recruit in agility, strength, endurance, and of course with fear. My hands were laced with sweat before beginning each obstacle and they are now as I write about this challenging time in my life. We formed up behind the company for the morning report, and with a right face we were off.

"Double time…. March!" was sounded. The recruits replied with a loud and thunderous "Marine Corps!" The running cadence sounded: "Lo, righty, Lo, righty, lo righty lay oh….."

I ran with my mates, my stomach already in knots for the challenges that lay just ahead.

"God, help me, please…" I whispered to myself.

Faith can make you feel comforted before walking in the valley of the shadow of death. I recited that Psalm several times in my head. The run was not long and soon the commands followed:

"Quick time… march! Mark, time, march!"

In my head, I chanted the dittys that aided in the learning of these drill movements: "Step, right leg, and up."

Following a short warm up, 1084 moved to the confidence course. Our voices sounded with powerful roars reminiscent of medieval battlefields long lost to the pages and dust of history. Hearing the roars of large bodies of armed men prepare for battle boils one's blood like nothing else. It prepares one to walk into the doors of chaos and perhaps certain death.

My platoon was separated into squads and positioned near different obstacles throughout the field. The first obstacle in my sights was called the "stairway to heaven." This structure was essential a gigantic ladder made of logs and 2x4s. It spanned to roughly 30 feet in the air and was wide enough for two men to climb side by side. Most recruits had little difficulty with the strength that it took to complete this one. However, the fear factor on this god-forsaken ladder was extreme.

I approached it and began my climb. My upper body strength had increased from the month of training so far and I found the climb easy. My hands were soaked in sweat and I did not attempt to even place my gaze to anywhere close to looking down. "God help me… God help me…" I continually whispered. I made it.

The confidence course is a wonderful analogy for the Marine psychology while you spend time on Parris Island. Every charge and victory is not rewarded with a rest or a good job. Instead, it was rewarded with another horribly difficult test. This mentality conditions one for war and its many mortal obstacles.

My squad charged the next objective. It was a four-level structure called the "Sky Scraper." It is essentially a building with flat floors every six to seven feet stacked one over the other. My squad worked as a team to beat this obstacle. To climb over a floor, one had to essentially grab the outside of the floor, do a pull-up while at the same time hooking your foot to the floor above. Shorter men, like myself had a harder time climbing than the others. However, I compensated with my strength in aiding the others to get to the next level.

One of the most dreaded obstacles on the field was called "The Tough One." The name itself did it full justice. I looked at this grotesque structure composed of ropes and logs with complete disdain in my heart.

"Fuck it," I said to myself.

By this point of the training, I had mastered (enough) the art of rope climbing. The first portion of this obstacle was a 15' rope climb. I established my footing, or what is called the bite, and pulled myself up hand over hand.

I made it up. The next portion involved walking over logs one foot after the other while being 20' suspended in the air. I did not want to do it, but I had to. I took a large gulp of this fear and swallowed it whole. I moved out and the 10-meter walk, moving from log to log felt like I was transcending a psychological marathon over the trail of fear. The obstacle ended with a further vertical climb and a rope climb down to the ground level. I was overjoyed to finish this one.

I continued this horrid day of training and successfully completed these trials made of wood and rope. The entire day I took shots of fear and gulped them down without hesitation. It was only after years, like everything else on Parris Island, that this sort of training made sense. Certainly, it conditioned us physically. However, that was not the goal. This obstacle course continued to build up an immunity toward the worst disease a warrior can ever face on the field of battle: fear. Parris Island continued ejecting this immunity on a daily basis. I was learning not to ignore fear, but to accept it.

FEAR

What is fear? The Greek fathers of western war studied this concept and called it the phobos, the son of Ares.

We make monsters to slaughter enemies on the fields of war. The problem is when they roam the glens of peace.

When you make monsters for war, how do we imagine they will function in the real world.

GAS CHAMBER

1084 marched into a very archaic classroom. Parris island was full of simple looking classrooms such as these. My platoon had been on the island for over a month now. I knew how to move quickly and respond to orders without hesitation. I could recite some of the greatest glories of Marine Corps heroics and history. Most of all, my platoon was learning how to both expect and take pain.

The nuclear, biological, and chemical (NBC) training began. Marine Corps Instructors are taught to utilize intensity in all their lessons. It is inherent in every type of Marine Corps Instructor, ranging from Close Combat Instructors, swimming, shooting, and even chemical Instructors. These NBC Instructors were no exception to the norm when they discussed the failure of what could occur in the event of a nerve agent attack. They told us that if we were too slow in responding to a chemical attack, we could die in a horrible manner. The death in particular would be caused by a spasm causing us to lose control over our bodies and breaking our own spine. None of us wanted to suffer such a fate and it made us pay attention to the remainder of the period of instruction.

I was taught the important indicators of an NBC attack. The most important thing to do in the event of an attack was to get my mask and chemical suit on as quickly as possible and to signal others by saying: "Gas, Gas, Gas!" while at the same time flapping my fingers up and down. The Instructors covered the use of the different medical kits and washing procedures in case of a nuclear attack.

I knew what was coming that day… the Gas chamber. Boot camp taught me that fear can be sensed easier when people are together in large groups. The fear was so thick that I can still taste it on my tongue as I write in the confines of a comfortable coffee shop.

I paid close attention to the use of the gas mask. Every aspect was taught with the strictest attention to detail possible. Attaining a proper seal was perhaps the most important aspect of this training. One started by tightening down the straps around the back of your head. Once your head was snugly secured in the mask, you pressed on the outlet valve and breathed out. Next you placed your hand on the air filter and breathed in. If the mask collapsed around your head when you breathed in, you achieved a correct seal on your mask.

The instruction portion was over and every man knew what was next: the gas chamber. 1084 formed up in straight lines and placed their masks on. The Marines wasted no time with us and members of the platoon immediately started to venture into this choking inferno.

I can still hear my shallow breaths going in and out within the small confines of my gas mask as I waited in line. The mask was my salvation from the upcoming suffocation ensured by the CS infested atmosphere of the gas chamber. I gazed at the front of the column, past them, and on to the doors of the chamber. The eyes of every recruit were pasted to those doors. Everyone knew that only pain waited behind them.

Finally, the doors to the chamber swung open. A light cloud of CS gas crawled out and with it, one of the Drill Instructors in full MOPP level IV (a full chemical suit). He came out and shouted for the first group of recruits to move into the chamber. I no longer question what the gates of hell must look like when one of hell's servants comes to force the lost souls into the inferno.

The recruits moved into the gas chamber, the door shut, and my place in line came closer to walking into this place of nightmares. I waited for what perhaps was only a few minutes, but seemed as if it lasted a lifetime. I constantly made sure that I had a tight seal on my mask. Finally, the door of the chamber swung open.

A group of recruits staggered out of the chamber, each of their faces stained with a primordial pain. Their arms were extended like in an airplane and in one hand was their mask. The men were hacking up all their mucus and most were yelling in intense pain.

Recruits continued to walk into and out of this hell. Before long, my group was next to walk in. My heart rate increased and with it my breathing. Soon, the door to the chamber swung open and beckoned me to walk into this torture chamber.

I marched in with my comrades and we were ordered to halt. The CS gas was very thick and obscured my vision. My skin burned due to the exposure of the heavily concentrated CS. The DIs ordered us to conduct a few exercises to increase our heart rate and breathing. My seal held, but a few of the recruits near me were not so fortunate. They had breathed in gas and began doing the dance known as "the funky Chicken"—a Marine euphemism for the frantic waving of one's hands due to pain.

"So far so good," I thought to myself. I eagerly awaited the next command.

"At this time, you will break your seal and expose your entire face."

1084 rehearsed these movements while in the classroom prior to entering the chamber. I dreaded this moment before it had occurred. Here we go.

I unmasked and attempted to hold my breath, like every other man in the chamber. We were then given the command to mask up again and attain our seal. Some of the gas entered my mouth as I was attempting to attain a seal.

What unfolded next was some of the most traumatizing and memorable pain that I ever felt in my life. The CS gas entered my lungs and it felt as if I was breathing in fire. I was suffocating in this pool filled with cloudy murky fire. I desperately tried to regain my seal and struggled.

Pain, if nothing else, reminds us that we are animals. Like a wounded animal stuck in a trap, I struggled to breathe, survive, and simply not die. I began doing the "funky chicken" and I was mad at myself for it. The "funky chicken is nothing to laugh at. A man flails his arms as if he is on fire from the pain. I was mad for losing control, but the pain seared my head and brought me to the shores of insanity. I always thought that I was above such silly stressors. But I found that was not the case.

Every instinct in my body told me to make a run for the door and to seek life giving air. However, this is where the discipline kicked in. My obedience to the orders of not to run superseded my natural and seemingly logical thoughts. The very tenets of going against one's own self preservation is essential for those in the profession of war. It was not logical to stay in this room breathing in fire. Years later, it would not be logical to stay in position while trading bullets with the enemy on the battlefields of Afghanistan. Such lessons are painful, however essential in the education of war.

It was only seconds that I was struggling in the chaos, but it felt like an eternity of gasping for relief. I needed help. Surprisingly, I was rescued by one of the makers of the chaos: my Senior Drill Instructor SSgt Telford.

He emerged from the corner of the room and shoved me against the wall.

"Relax, recruit!" he shouted in my face.

He swiftly placed his hand on my mask's outlet valve.

"Clear your mask!"

I violently exhaled the fiery air from my lungs.

SSgt Telford moved his hand to the air filter.

"Breathe in!"

I listened to him and I took a deep breath of filtered air into my lungs. I was saved from the ensuing chaos. This was another example of the paternal code amongst Marine leaders, especially the SDI. His cool orders rescued me from the chaos.

This hell was not over just yet. With tears in my eyes, I continued to take taxing breaths under the protection of my mask. SSgt Telford continued observing me from afar. My head pounded with hot air and my ears were tortured from the screams of the other sufferers in this chamber of pain. The training continued.

The order to unmask was then given. The gas entered my lungs as the door to the gas chamber swung open, and emitted sunlight into the depths of this torture chamber. The CS ignited my lungs and my head pounded. I wanted to sprint out of this chamber. However, I knew that this was not an option. Instead, I accepted the pain and continued my slow walk outside the chamber.

The other tortured souls and I made it outside the gas chamber, gagging and yelling in extreme agony. I coughed out the CS and screamed in misery. I wanted to fall on the ground and moan in pain. I would have, if I had experienced this off of Parris Island. I used what little bearing that I still had within me and kept walking.

The experience of the gas chamber is shared misery between the Army and the Marines. I have often asked NBC specialists as to why we must take off masks in the Gas chamber. They insist it is to instill confidence in the equipment. I have a different theory.

Nothing teaches a lesson like pain does. I think we were given this experience to mimic the feeling of the death that could occur in the event of a real chemical or nerve agent in battle. At the time of the training, it truly did feel like I was going die. The very idea or thought of the gas chamber will bring about anxiety and even fear to Marines and soldiers alike.

I have been wounded by an IED and have broken my leg on

a jump from a C-17. However, the gas chamber still has been one of the most painful moments in my life.

Most of the brutal effects of the gas left my system after only five minutes or so. I was in line with my comrades to wash out my mask. My eyes were mostly open at the time. SSgt Telford approached me.

"Did you die, Salinas?"

"No, Sir!" I answered.

"Well, you sure as hell looked like you were going to."

"Yes, Sir!"

I could see the humor in the eyes of this hardened warrior. He moved away and he forever became a part of the tapestry of my warrior mind.

RAPPELLING

The Marines continued to shock my system with becoming accustomed to fear. However, the application of being comfortable with heights is not merely for psychological hardening alone. Rather, it has a practical application. Marines are expected to conduct a large slew of operations ranging from standard woodland patrols, to fast roping and rappelling from helicopter platforms in swift operations, often starting from the sea.

The rappelling tower is a 60-foot platform with a smooth wooden wall. I felt the fear creep within my gut when I laid my eyes on the towering structure. However, something was different somehow about it. The fear beaded down on me like the hot sun upon my skin. I felt it, like the heat of the South Carolina sum-

mer. However, that day I did something different. I did something there that I had not done before. I simply accepted the fear.

When one conducts patrols in a hot environment, you learn
to accept the ever-present fear and debilatating heat. Your body
accepts the warmth and sweats in an attempt to cool itself. The
training and the practice of the art of war are similar in many
respects. Fear was always constant, both on the island and in the
valleys of war. The fear has a permanent place in the atmosphere
and never leaves. In Parris Island, the fear was in the scent of my
sweat and in the dust we breathed during road marches. It was
never absent from my world.

I prepared myself and looked to preparing the infamous Swiss
seat necessary for rappelling operations. I focused on the orders
in tying this knot round my body. I ensured that it had the necessary space for the carabineer to fit. Focus is the counter to fear
I soon came to find.

The path to the top of the rappelling tower was a long stair-
case with a switchback every six stairs or so. It was my first time
attempting to completely suppress the fear. I had a blank look on
my face. It was a look that I would later see on the faces of other
men who became desensitized to fear engendered violence. I saw
this same look on the Pashtuns in Kunar's Pech river valley, Afghanistan. For only an instant I learned how animals such as the
wildebeest possess the ability to drink water, only a few feet from
the crocodiles in rivers of Africa.

I made it to the top of the tower and tried with the best of
my ability not to make eye contact with other recruits whose gaze
unmistakably reeked of fear. I waited for my turn. The rappelling
Instructor looked me in the eyes. He knew that I was doing my
best to be brave and cracked a subtle smile when our eyes met.

"Just listen, do what I say, and you'll be fine, recruit," he said.

"Yes, sir."

The lean Instructor fed the rope through my carabineer with his tanned and powerful appearing arms. I placed my hand on the rope and shouted: "Front hand lead hand, back hand-brake hand. Recruit Salinas on Rappel."

The recruit below me shouted: "On belay."

My eyes were locked with the Instructor as I backed my heels over the edge of the rappel tower. The thing about fear is that no matter how desensitized you think you might be, the feeling of dread never completely goes away. It remains like a stubborn undying ember from a drenched camp fire.

"Keep your legs straight, recruit," the Instructor said.

Carefully, I walked backwards over the side. I kept my legs straight and my body at 90 degrees. I was ordered to move. I kicked my body away from the wall while simultaneously releasing my brake hand off the small of my back. For a brief second, I was in the air and all fear left me as I swung back to the wall. I continued rappelling lower and lower until I was at the ground. I made it. Holy fuck.

While on the island, fear was given to us like a protein shake. It is mixed together and given to recruits, like a weightlifter takes his supplements. Fear to the untrained can be a debilitating substance, making them incapable of action or movement. It can do this to warriors untested in battle as well. Men who have tasted battle for the first time can at times freeze up and become unable to move. They take their strong sip of this horrid tonic, cringe their face, and instead wait for horrible death to take them deep into the dark.

As a recruit, I learned to gorge myself on this brutal tonic. I allowed it to seep deep into my blood vessels and allow my muscles to expand for the reaping of the enemy. I felt my pre-workout buzz and took it in strongly. I fed on this fear as if it was a steroid.

I became enraged and smiled at the devastation that I will shortly give out to my unlucky foes. Here at Parris Island, I almost became desensitized to this buzz. It got to the point that I almost needed this horrid serum to function.

The Marines have found a way mass produce this liquid and inject it into a recruit's veins. It is the only other place on Earth where I have found this fear driven high, other than combat. If you ever visit my island either for training or as a tourist, you will feel it as well. Like the first time you visit the hallowed fields of Gettysburg, the feel of the place speaks to your soul.

There are certain places on the earth that speak to all warriors throughout the earth. The inherit screams and pain shed upon the folds of the earth there will forever sing of their pain. Parris Island is one of these places that eternally sings of its pain. Be warned.

SENIOR DRILL INSTRUCTOR INSPECTION

The tenets of intensity, fear, and attention to detail make up the entire fabric of the atmosphere at Parris Island. I arrived at the island as a mere rough Neanderthal statue of what a warrior should look like. These Drill Instructors tirelessly hacked away the soft stone of which my body was made. Through sweat, through horrible yells, and through pain, they made me closer to the ideal of a warrior.

Pain is the river which cuts deep canyons into the memory of those who practice war. Pain is one of the dominant shaping factors in this profession of hunting man. Warriors carry these scars, whether visible or not, for the entirety of their lives. These lessons imprint into you with the slam of an IED, the boom of an RPG, or that horrid whip-snap of a bullet. They are never forgotten. I learned the horrible cost of pain first hand on the battlefield. However, I first felt this pain on both the sand and soil on Parris Island, South Carolina.

This river of pain can take many forms in the lecture halls in this university of war. The panting during a forced march or during an unarmed contest with another Marine recruit may be easily understood. However, the pain given off by the booming voice of a Drill Instructor, a mere inches from one's face, is perhaps one of the most difficult to comprehend to the casual observer. It is also perhaps the most forceful of shaping mechanisms on this island of war.

When a Marine Drill Instructor corrects a recruit, his voice covers him like the heat of a raging forest fire. In his voice, he carries the many centuries of rage and anger motivated leadership earned from the Halls of Montezuma to the streets of Fallujah and the fields of Helmand. He carries Death in his voice. This shocking leadership voice resonated in one's soul. If you are Marine, you know what this means. You may even know what it means, if you have had the misfortune to piss a Marine off.

I had been on island for nearly a month now and received word that the various Senior Drill Instructors from our company would inspect my platoon. Inspections are one of the oldest forms of examining troops; particularly within in the early stages of their development. To the untrained eye, it may appear that standing erect before a senior warrior, with a pretty, well groomed uniform has little to do in preparing a man for battle. Nothing could be further from the truth.

Even after surviving the trials of battle, the idea of an inspection can bring chills to many Marines. What is it that drives so much anxiety behind these inspections? It is the fear of receiving this intense backlash of violence-laced degradation from one of these Drill Instructors.

INSPECTION PREPARATION

I hunted for these horrible despicable objects on my uniform known as Irish pennants. These are the loose strands of string hanging off seams. I was issued a pair of cuticle scissors, not that the Marines were necessarily concerned about the manicure condition of my hands. Rather, these cuticle scissors were used to hunt these straggling little pieces of string. I spent hours hunting for them and cutting them off.

Irish pennants or spare hanging pieces of string are normal in the regular world ruled by civilian sheep. I am certain that if you were to look down upon the very shirt you are wearing you could find a few of these. They are normal and a part of the civilian world that all of us warriors come from. However, here in the academy og sea borne warriors, they had no place.

These pennants, like many other norms in the civilian world, had no place here on these training grounds on the shores of hell's ocean. I left them and other such intricacies of normalcy outside this place. I left all those things behind, safely tucked away in our safe homelands. I left my girlfriend, family, and perhaps my innocence at the front gate of the island.

Marines view the world in shades of darkness. Sometimes, I do not observe the world in a promising bright warm light. This attention to detailed training during uniform prep taught me to study something much different in the light of day. I began noticing the shadows; it was in the shadows that I found my home. It is this darkness that all warriors and Marines have within them. This art form flowers in the heat of battle, where warriors seek to bring death to their adversaries. Warriors hunger for the hunt. The problem many Marines experience is when they no longer have to prowl in the darkness and join the land of the living again. Can angels of Death ever walk in the light of day?

I spent hours upon hours grooming my uniforms, weapons, and my mind for this upcoming inspection from my Senior Drill Instructor.

SSgt Telford looked exactly the way I would have expected one of Caesar's centurions of his famed 10th legion would have. He was around my height, around 5'6." His body looked as if it was crafted from stone, but dirtied by the winds carrying the sand of war. He did not carry love handles. Warriors in my profession have no need for such reserves of fat.

As a young recruit, I noticed that there was something overly compelling about this man's eyes. Back then, I wondered what could give a man such an ability to stare into my soul and touch my deepest fears. That summer, I assumed that it was as a consequence of being a Marine and a Drill Instructor for years on end. It would be over a decade later where I learned the origin of such a look.

SSgt Telford had the "look" of combat. I knew that he had fought in Somalia and the Gulf in the early 90's, but I had no idea what that truly meant. After tasting combat myself, I think back to the way that he looked at me. His look seemed to be amplified by the color of his gray eyes. When he looked at me, it was like staring at some ancient stain glassed windows, whose stains came from the strongest of granite.

All Drill Instructors had a certain look of intensity, regardless if they had combat experience or not. However, SSgt Telford's intensity had a level unique to its own. I was held captive by his eyes, like a deer in the headlights.

My fellow recruits and I continued in our preparation to be inspected and questioned by these modern-day centurions.

My modern spear, my M16 A2 service rifle demanded special attention. I spent hours conducting rifle maintenance and I did it in the manner that would make sacrament masters of the Vatican, or Bonsai professionals smile. I was issued a special cleaning rag that had labels and pictures of the various portions of my rifle.

BREAKING DOWN THE RIFLE AND CLEANING

To a Marine, disassembling a rifle is a sacred time. Somehow it made me feel more vulnerable. I undressed her slowly and carefully during this process. I did it slowly, as not to lose any of her vital parts. I caressed her carefully and slowly as to not harm her.

I started by pushing out the disassembly bolt between the upper and lower receiver. The upper disassembly bolt follows this. Once complete, I separated the upper and lower receiver. I gently placed them onto the cleaning rag. Next, I take hold of the charging handle, and gently pulled out the bolt. I separate the charging handle from bolt. I move next the bolt and use my index finger to slide out the retaining pin, allowing the firing pin to fall out. I separated the bolt. Next I moved back to the upper receiver and took off what at times could be the very tricky rifle handgrips. The process was almost complete and I moved back to the lower receiver. I pushed in the buffer spring, while at the same time suppressing the button. I pulled it out and it was ready.

Rifle cleaning must be done with utmost care, patience, and skill. The humid air on Parris Island can create rust on the rifle in just a small matter of time. For hours on end, I scrubbed the rifle to remove any semblance of dirt or rust. Small traces of carbon, from the last time the rifle was fired still hung desperately on the bolt and barrel. I took special care to cleaning my blades for war.

INSPECTION DAY

1084 was awake, fed, and PTed. I was given another chance to shave, ensuring my face was clean for inspection. Being of Latin decent, growing facial hair became one of my favorite curses of life. No matter how carefully I shaved, I knew that there would be a random piece of hair upon my face. Getting gigged for this offense was something that I learned to deal with.

I dressed for inspection in my carefully pressed cammies and clean weapons. These inspections were conducted indoors; which at least saved the recruits from the searing summer heat. On both sides of the squad bay, 1084 formed up and stood at parade rest. The Charlie Company SDIs strode into the squad bay. It began.

Although, this was somewhat of a formal affair, it began like everything else did on this island. It began with intensity and yelling. I attempted to keep my eyes to the front and stare just above the eyes of the recruit across from me.

It was difficult to remain focused and unshaken by the surrounding chaos. I felt like a wildebeest attempting to remain silent, while a horde of lions was tearing other members of my herd into shreds. Years later I realized the useful application of this experience to the battlefield. In modern warfare, the battlefield can engulf an entire front. However, this does not necessarily mean that every unit within earshot of the action will be engaged.

There have been times at war where I was the reserve or quick reaction force leader. You can hear machine gun fire both audibly and over the radio. Every piece of you wants to run full into the fray and take part of the action. It is a natural instinct; and sometimes can bring much needed support to the element in contact. However, at other times you can make the situation worse by adding more chaos to the fire.

Resisting the urge to add yourself to the chaos is certainly a difficult aspect to teach, learn, and far more difficult to implement. Few things are more valuable in a contest of arms than an unbloodied unit held in reserve then later unleashed at the critical moment in battle.

Waiting for the inspection is an excellent example of that important aspect known as tactical patience. I felt like a British riflemen from the 18th century, holding my spot in line and attempting not to break ranks, nor allow my bayonet to shake worriedly in the air. I held my position and waited to be called to attention. The order finally arrived.

I held at attention, attempting not to lock my knees and to constantly mentally rehearse the movement of inspection arms. The pack of Drill Instructors drew ever closer to my position. Although, I was in the confines of air conditioning; I could not prevent the beads of sweat forming upon my forehead and my arms, a gift formed from the anticipation of the approaching inspection.

The dark shadow lurked next to me. My turn had arrived. SSgt Telford conducted a sharp right face and gazed directly into my eyes. It began...

I initiated my performing of the movement called inspection

arms. I said the movement to myself in my head: "One and two... bringing me to port arms. I then slid my left arm to the pistol grip, while at the same time touching the bolt grip button. My right hand pulled the charging handle and locked it to the rear. I returned the charging handle back to its home. I moved the rifle to my left side and ensured the chamber was empty of any rounds. The rifle was ready. SSgt Telford aggressively grabbed the rifle from my grip and began inspecting it.

The point of an inspection is to get your ass kicked. Even if the rifle had been cleaned for six months straight and then kept in an airless vacuum, the Drill Instructors could still find a fault in it. They always did. He asked me questions such as: "Did you even clean this weapon?" Of course I answered with "Sir, yes, Sir!" The ridicule over my weapon continued for a few moments longer. He returned the weapon and I moved to order arms.

"Improper shave." He said to me and his scribe recorded it.

The Drill Instructor continued and he was relentless in his attack upon me.

"What's your first general order?" he asked.

"Sir, this recruit's first general order is to take charge of this post and all government property in view."

The test continued and finally he was done with me.

Inspections are a brutal but a necessary test to ensure that a warrior will not shatter under the horrible stress of combat. In battle, one is collided with a barrage of stressors ranging from pain, fatigue, and noise. Combat covers you with an intense heat and a sorrow-ridden blanket. You enter this hurricane of death, violence, and pain. Scholarly warriors such as Clausewitz have done well to coin the term, "Fog of war."

"Fog of war" is an accurate statement and in no way am I attempting to degrade this father of warfare. However, for those who have been in direct contact with the enemy, the confusion and chaos does not slowly roll in like some coastal fog. Rather, it slams you like a tornado shattering the fields of humanity.

The training on Parris Island is in fact brutal. However, the lessons learned under the confusion of battle are much more severe. The harder the training, the less death will occur on your side in actual combat. It is a hard truth that all combat veterans have learned. Everything on Parris Island is done for a reason. Among the many reasons, they are done for one most important one: they are to keep Marines alive in battle.

PHASE 1 IN REVIEW

The first phase of Parris Island is amongst the most memorable moments in a Marine's life. Young Marine recruits are immersed into this orchestra of violence, pain, fear, and obedience—even before setting one foot on the island. By the time we make it to those legendary yellow footprints, our souls are lit aflame to a new world whose heartbeat flows with the blood of intensity.

This shock and intensity learned on the island are the very aspects that provide magic, to the word "Marine." Many people have asked in years gone by how physically demanding boot camp really is. It is designed so that an average young male or woman can succeed in graduating. What makes the training at Parris Island difficult is not necessarily that they run faster or longer than any of the services. Rather, it is that the intangible tenets of respect, obedience, and intensity are burned into the souls of all Marines, regardless of MOS (Military Occupational Specialty or job).

By the end of first phase, Marine recruits have a good grasp of what in God's name being a Marine actually means. Many would call this type of training brainwashing. It is not. This training is designed to forge very hard warriors to excel in the art, theory, and practice of war.

The thing a Marine recruit learns early on is that you have to, above all, want to be a Marine. It is this desire that kept me and all others that have earned the Eagle, Globe, and Anchor in this profession of arms for so long.

This desire is what permits one to make it through recruit training and take all the degradations from the masters of war who wear the Eagle Globe and Anchor around their waists. It is this desire that goes beyond the simple tenets of feeling patriotic and feeling compelled to serve one's country. It is this call to become a warrior and serve with the best ones on the face of the Earth.

PHASE II

Marine recruits are forced to mature quickly on the plains of Mars. My body was learning and adapting to a new language... a language of war. All of 1084 was learning together. The recruits moved as wolf cubs, watching the impressive timber wolves powerfully stride on the sands of Iwo Jima. With the passing of each day my knowledge of war and of hunting man continued to enhance.

The constant companions of pain, misery, volume, and intensity were present in every stage of the training. Each morning, 1084 was dressed for war in the same chaotic fashion as when boot camp first began: Lights! Lights! And the count off. There was one such occasion where I was able to observe this chaos as an outsider.

FIREWATCH, 0400-0500

A companion and I drew fire watch together. Typically fire watch began in the darkness and ended in the same fashion. It was different this time. My fire watch shift ended with the beginning of the training day.

I walked my tour, marching down the lonely hall of the squad bay and the head. It was quiet, and I was alone with my thoughts, thinking of girls and freedom. I walked by myself, alone with my thoughts, in the manner that all warriors do while on guard. It was a sacred and quiet time that many warriors cherish.

Learning to be a disciplined guard is an important factor to military operations. These Marines would one day pull guard duty in ancient Mesopotamia and Afghanistan behind a 240B, M249s, or the famous M2 machine gun. Here they would stare off long moments into the darkness, looking for an enemy that may or may not attack.

I remembered my lonely guard tours of my own when I visited my men on guard on my rustic outpost in Afghanistan. I approached them in the night, walking up into the tower. I entered the guard shack and looked into their eyes. I looked into their eyes and felt warm to see what I saw. It was the look of trust and faith. The same faith and trust that I had in my father to teach me how to shoot or to drive without fear across the country.

Walking a guard post teaches you paternal responsibility. Like myself, many warriors practice the art of making of life for years on end. They wonder if they ever could in fact become fathers. However, they have proven that they, in fact, already have to their comrades in the horrid practice of war.

At 0430, I walked to the DI hut and banged on the piece of wood which had a large yellow hand painted on it. The last fire watches acted as the alarm clock for the DI on duty that night. "Good morning, Sir! The time on deck is 0430." The Drill Instructor replied: "Go away, recruit, and don't come back."

The banging on the door had stirred me from sleep on a few occasions. A few recruits rustled in their beds prepping themselves for the chaos, which was to unfold shortly. We are not permitted to carry wristwatches while training. However, there was a clock on the quarterdeck. I saw the time was 0450 and that the chaos would soon unfold.

The DIs arrived and prepared their storm. The intensity of dressing never lost its thrill. It brought chills to my spine each time. The shock of the morning lights ceremony shocked my system like an exploding 155 howitzer every time. The other recruit on fire watch took his place on his position on the quarterdeck with me. The DIs marched out of their huts like proud masters of the island that they were.

"Lights! Lights! Get on line... You got 10,9,8....!" They screamed. I stood there as a rare observer to this ceremony, like a person watching the running of the bulls might do in Spain. It was a grotesque theatre to look upon my comrades attempting to shake off their sleepy haze. The Drill Instructors descended upon them like predators killing purely for the thrill of the hunt. It was a horribly beautiful sight and I felt fortunate to watch this manifestation of chaos in the controlled medium of Parris Island.

The Drill Instructors were relentless in their practice of making Marines. They are truly the gatekeepers of chaos on this land where few men dare to roam. I felt bad for these drowsy recruits in their first few moments of consciousness. It was a savagely beautiful sight to behold and one that shall forever be burned into the pages of my warrior soul.

INITIAL DRILL

Drill was practiced each and every day. It dictated how we moved from place to place on the island. We never walked. Rather we moved swiftly and sharply to every location in and around base.

Each march was an example of the skill of the DIs who trained us with every piece of fabric and will that was available within their bodies.

My company's first drill competition was approaching and was on the minds of all the recruits and Drill Instructors in the company. Most of 1084's free moments were used to sharpen our response to commands and flow. We practiced each time with the sharpness one may expect to see at the changing of the guard on Arlington cemetery in Washington D.C.

1084 marched to the parade deck and were swiftly moved to the bleachers. My mates and I watched the other platoons on their parades and the observing Drill Masters who were in charge of grading this demonstration of western militaries.

It was my platoon's turn and we moved to the battlefield. It began, and I felt even more intensity and pride flow through each member of the platoon in drill. We marched sharply and power-fully upon the field as if we were squaring up to do battle on the plains of Europe facing Frederick's famous Prussians.

1084 scored averagely but we were not punished by the Drill Instructors. Rather we were further inspired by the DI to strive to do better on the drill field the next time we were ordered upon the Parade field.

The Marines whom we were placed under their charge worked amazingly well to both train us for war but also inspire a broth-erhood of trust and shared misery within all of us in the platoon. It is within the wasted bandages soaked in sweat and blood that true brotherhood is created.

INITIAL CLOTHING ISSUE

I was beginning to look, talk, and feel like a Marine. I could march almost like one of these wolves that commanded us in this symphony of war. No longer, did 1084 have to recite those silly ditties to remember the marching commands and drill movements as junior recruits. Rather, the recruits were functioning in the way that Drill had intended us to.

Drill takes the thinking out of it. The recruits executed commands without hesitation or worry. The timber wolves howled and I knew exactly what to do. The recruits moved toward the sounds of the howls as we would one day move to the sound of the guns. The eternal call of war brought us closer and closer to being United States Marines.

The halfway point of the training cycle loomed ever near. I still had many trials to overcome. However, I continued to move forward ever deeper into the high winds of this unholy tempest of war. As one does in a storm, I kept my head down and took the winds. In this dark night, I received a glimmer of hope I think we all needed. I was given an early remainder of the glory that lay only a few months ahead upon the Parade field. 1084 was given a taste.

That morning, 1084 marched near the receiving barracks. I had visited this place a few times since arriving to the island, to get haircuts. The smell of this place brought back those horrid memories of my first few hours on the island. This part of the island holds some of the highest concentration of Marine Corps Magic. 1084 marched into a large warehouse that held the uniforms of United States Marines. They held the glory that each recruit sought.

PHOTO

My squad moved upstairs and away from the tailors. I entered a room and it was soon apparent what we were in for. The room was adorned with a single camera and coat racks that may have held all the gold of the famed El Dorado. My mouth hung open in awe and that special flame called hope burned every brighter in my heart. Marine Dress blues hung there.

These Dress blues make up the iconic photos that remain burned into the minds of Marines and Marine hopefuls for the entirety of their lives. Hope is as powerful of a catalyst for action as pain is. When the two are combined in the proper way, as it is on the Island, the results are epic.

These Dress blues touch me and sang so many lovely secrets into my warrior heart.

Are you worthy of me?
How bad do want to wear me?
Do you want to hear of glory?
What is it that you want?

If you win, you wear me
You will become strength, honor, and vitality
It won't be long
Move to the sound of the guns…

That moment, as I looked in awe at the black uniforms with red trim, gold buttons, and the coveted Eagle, Globe, and Anchors was one of the most inspiring capsules of time for me on the island. It emboldened my effort to win and to become a United States Marine.

These Dress Blue tops were not the proper ones we would later wear in the fleet. Rather, they were half the top and had an open back. They were for photos only. It did not matter. The thing that people don't realize about Marine recruits is that they so desperately want to become Marines. Recruits want this title more than a breath of air while you are submerged underneath water. This title becomes your breath, want, and desire. This is why Marines change so much when they graduate from this island. This title is everything.

These half-tailored uniforms were as good as the real thing for me. I thought that if they are spending the time to take my photo, I at least had a chance at graduating. I stood in line waiting for my turn to be fitted and approach the photographer's backdrop. I watched with envy as the recruits in front of me were dressed in these blues and were adorned with the Marine Corps dress blue cover (hat).

I could sense the pride ignite within the soul of every man in the room. I watched my comrades march in front of the photographer's backdrop. They stared at the camera in a way that I had never seen or will forget in my entire life. They stared with intensity as if they were staring into the gates of hell. They looked not at the photographer, but somehow into the beyond. You can see it for yourself if you take the time to stare at a Marine's photo. For a brief second, you too will be able to see into the beyond and see this glory that is promised by the Marines.

My turn was fast approaching and a civilian contractor approached me. She fitted me with the tight form fitting dress blue top, followed by my cover. Chills and energy unknown to me before flowed throughout the entirety of my body. "Holy fuck. This is really happening."

I was up and ordered to turn to the camera. Without being

told, I gave the look of intensity that I knew I had to for such a sacred and powerful moment. I looked into the camera with the power of a thousand rifles pouring lead unto the enemy. I looked at the camera like the Marine that I wanted to be.

My eyes became the dark soulless of a predator like a Great White Shark. It was almost as if I could feel the souls of warriors long lost to the accounts of history flow through my body. Although, I was not yet a United States Marine, I felt the power assist my heart to pulse with life and fire. I became that warrior.

Me posing for my Marine photo.

UNIFORMS

My group and I were ushered back downstairs, with hearts pounding with pride. I thought that if they were spending so much effort on pictures and uniforms then surely we were getting closer to graduating. Regardless if this was true or not, it maintained that essential element which give people the ability to endure through horrible agonies and continue well past the point of endurance: hope.

Hope can fill all the dark voids of despair that exists within the human heart. Hope helps to maintain all those cold places within my soul. Understanding, creating, and shaping hope is essential for military leaders at all levels. A man without hope is a dangerous and nearly uncontrollable animal.

Civilian tailors were in charge of taking measurements and it was one of the few times on island where recruits are treated like human beings. I stood up on a large wooden platform and was measured from head to toe for my uniform. I loved trying on the class "A" green top uniform in particular. 1084 was soon finished with this clothing ritual and we were marshaled outside, again in formation.

It was impossible not to sense the feeling of pride that hung around my platoon like a thick spring morning fog. Each man in the formation stuck his chest out a bit further and straightened his shoulders. This day, we felt for a few brief moments what it was like to have the honor of wearing the Eagle Globe and Anchor. This pride was intoxicating, and Marines carry this pride for all their days on Earth.

RIFLE RANGE

My Rifle
The creed of a United States Marine
By Major General W. H. Rupertus

This is my rifle. There are many like it, but this one is mine.

My rifle is my best friend. It is my life. I must master it as I must master my life.

My rifle without me is worthless. Without my rifle, I am useless. I must fire my rifle true. I must shoot him before he shoots me. I will.

My rifle and myself know that what counts in this war is not the rounds we fire, the noise of my burst, nor the smoke we make. We know that it is the hits that count. We will hit...

My rifle is human, even as I, because it is my life. Thus, I will learn it as a brother. I will learn its weaknesses, its strengths, its parts, its accessories, its sights, and its barrel. I will ever guard it against the ravages of weather and damage. I will keep my rifle clean and ready, even as I am clean and ready. We will become part of each other. We will...

Before God I swear this creed. My rifle and myself are the defenders of my country. We are the masters of my enemy. We are the saviors of my life.

So be it, until victory is America's and there is no enemy, but Peace!

GRASS WEEK

I have shot rifles all my life, hunting in the forests of Michigan. Prior to my education on the training grounds of Parris Island;

I thought of shooting as a rather simple affair. To me, shooting involved little more than pointing at a target, holding my breath, pulling a trigger, and hoping for the best. I thought of shooting as a brute merely aiming and shooting. The Marines shattered my relatively simple concept of shooting.

Few things are more sacred to the Marines than marksmanship. To the Marines at Parris Island, there is no such thing as merely throwing rounds down range. Each round delivered is a highly calculated, precision-guided munition. One would think you were using JDAMs (Joint Direct Attack Munitions) at the rifle range and not 5.56 NATO ball. Marines taught the practice of marksmanship as one might teach Kung Fu in the legendary Shaolin temples.

FIELD AND MARKSMANSHIP TRAINING DIVISION

It was time to move to a new barracks. 1084 completed what it had to do to make it to the next level of training. As rough as life was in the main side barracks, it had become my home. This "H" shaped building became my place of refuge from the horrible heat of the South Carolina summer sun. It was my home. It was where I wrote letters to my girlfriend and mom. It was all I had.

The recruits packed up everything that was issued, save footlockers. My ALICE pack and sea bags were full. The Sea bags were staged and placed into a large truck.

1084 arrived out to this new foreign land. I grew accustomed to the life and routine at 1st Recruit Training Battalion. It was a viscous cycle of pain, drill, drill, pain, and PT. However, it was a cycle and at least knowing what I was in for provided at least some comfort. This new training ground composed the unknown for me. The thick fog of doubt and the unknown began to roll in like the swamp gas nearby 1st Battalion.

The Drill Instructors at Parris Island have an ingenious method of dispensing utter chaos and intensity at every moment. Simple administrative tasks that left gaps in the training cycles were filled with episodes of sheer chaos and madness.

We entered the barracks with the horrible heavy loads consisting of full ALICE packs, sea bags, and rifles. My load felt around 100 lbs or so. This opportunity was almost too much for my masters to pass up. The load was feeling heavy upon my frame and I wanted to desperately drop my burden. I was in store for something much more different than I was expecting.

"Keep moving recruits! Up the ladder well! (Stairs)"

We moved through the open squad bay and up the stairs. There was no sound at first, but we soon began howling out of exhaustion and replying to the DI's several horrible orders. We continued up and down the ladder wells of this small four-story tower to hell. My muscles burned, demanding relief as the sweat began to drip down my brow.

There was no relief in sight and we continued to push. The recruits around me continued to scream. I did not yield to this horrible pain. Rather, I chose to overcome the pain. I became a part of the incessant never ending wave of human violence. The Drill Instructors used historical references to keep us motivated during our ascent and descent in this tower of hell.

"Remember the Marines at Iwo Jima and Belleau Wood! Do you think they gave up their attacks when they were exhausted?? No! Keep moving recruits! I want to see pain recruits! Marines have been as tired as you are… and guess what?? They won battles!"

Even then, I was an aspiring historian and I found the DI's words to be truly inspiring. I strengthened my resolve and continued to push myself over the brink of exhaustion. Warriors and athletes alike know this feeling all too well. You have to make a choice when you finally meet this point of exhaustion. The easy choice is surrender. The hard choice is to continue to push beyond your limits.

The difference in war can be life or death.

The Marines foster this perseverance mentality of pushing into folds of hell without rest, mercy, or remorse. My mates and I charged like huge waves of water toward a smoldering shore, knowing full well its heat may vaporize us without remorse. This aggressive and violent wind is what makes contact possible amongst ancient and even modern day armies. It is this horrible gift harvested from the toils of young men that makes battle possible. This wind enables warriors to move past this fog of war into the jaws of certain death and destruction. We walk with heads held high and blades gleaming. We move through all this pain in hopes of finding this object known as victory. We push and push.

GRASS WEEK

Learning to yield death with a rifle is perhaps the most sacred rite passed down from Marines to recruits on the island. Teaching to kill with the rifle is a slow, highly detailed, and unforgettable process. The Marines use rifles as if they were miniature Michelangelo's using their paintbrushes. We were pupils and made ourselves ready for the remainder of this academic experience.

Marine Recruits spend an entire week learning and practicing weapon safety, positions, and the principles of marksmanship. Recruits further their mastery in marksmanship for hours into days under the hot sun, before even a single round of live ammunition is issued. The rifle no longer was this object of burden, whose weight tugged at me during humps. Instead, I learned to utilize its secrets to unlock the mystery of battle.

The rifle no longer was this simple spear I used during my daily parades or bayonet courses. 1084 began increasing practice time to use these rifles to rehearse the art of taking life. I started to learn to harvest the lives of men and to protect our way of life. This immense power of shredding my fellow man was taught with the utmost respect and diligence. Recruits first had to learn how to safely employ the safety lessons of this weapon.

Recruits chant all things learned on the island. The weapon safety rules were no exception:

1. Treat every weapon as if it were loaded.
2. Never point your weapon at anything you do not intend to shoot.
3. Keep your finger straight and off the trigger until you are ready to fire.
4. Keep the weapon on safe until you intend to fire.

I can still recite all these rules without fail, even now after nearly fifteen years from being on the island. My platoon recited all these rules in a rhythmic chant during the days at the field training battalion. Rules such as these may seem like common sense and very easy to follow. However, as Clausewitz stated, everything in war in simple and the simplest things are difficult.

CORRECTIVE TRAINING

Carrying an empty rifle is a fairly easy task to do. One carries it with some respect. However, once you enter the storm of combat or a rifle range, the atmosphere changes from a sunny calm day to a storm that lives and breathes violence. A rifle becomes something much different in the presence of live ammunition. It becomes that reaper blade only seen in nightmares.

1084 returned one evening to the barracks following a hot and sweaty day of marksmanship training. I was particularly tired that day and forgot some of the hard learned lessons of rifle discipline. All warriors know the effects of fatigue. It is a mishap that can perhaps betray you for only a few seconds. Consequently, a bullet needs only but a fraction of a second to spill a man's blood unto the earth. Fatigue can turn perfectionists into slobs. Parris Island however, has a control for such human weakness, they were the always hyper alert Drill Instructors.

That evening I entered the barracks following an afternoon PT session. My body was drenched in sweat and I felt myself succumbing to the effects of early heat exhaustion. For some reason, I did not drink as much water as I probably should have earlier that day. The animal in you becomes awakened when you are suffering the effects of exhaustion. I wanted nothing more than to take my web gear and rifle off my body and lay down.

Lazily, I unslung my rifle and the barrel carelessly flagged (pointed at) a few recruits for perhaps a half a second. To the uneducated eye, this infraction may seem only a simple mistake. However, those that have seen the effects of a 5.56mm bullet on a human body know the gravity of this potentially costly mistake. In battle, I later learned that the difference between life and death is measured in milliseconds and inches. A single misplaced trigger pull can send a ballistic round ripping through flesh, muscle, and bone.

A bullet is the perfect killer, once unleashed from a barrel, she will kill whoever you want her to. She will not take sides. She will shred a friend or enemy alike. She will not hold back once you pull the trigger. She will hunt down your target with unprecedented speed with a howl seemingly emitted from the depths of hell. She will slam into your target no matter what. There is no stopping her and the Drill Instructors knew it. I committed my infraction in plain view of SSgt Telford. I did not even realize that I had done it; until I made eye contact with him. By then I knew it was too late.

SSgt Telford peered into my soul with his gray stone eyes. His gaze penetrated even deeper than ever before. I felt the fear creep in, as he began to charge toward me. It was beginning:

"What are you doing, recruit!" I had no chance to respond and I am not sure what I would have said if I had the chance.

"You just killed those recruits there! I will have to write their mothers a letter because of what you did! Do you have any idea what one of these bullets can do to a person?"

"No, Sir!" I replied with fear in my veins.

"I have seen it, recruit! Trust me, it is not something you want to see on a fellow Marine!"

My education into this matter continued on the Drill Instructors favorite lecture hall: the quarterdeck. I was reminded of my mistake and the human cost that could have occurred as a result of it. Within minutes, sweat began making small ponds on the quarterdeck. I continued answering the Drill Instructors horrible questions by pitifully screaming, "Yes Sir! Yes Sir!" with what little breath still existed in pockets of my lungs.

This lesson was particularly painful. Although my body and

cardiovascular ability carried the brunt of this punishment, this punishment was not only for me. Rather, the lesson was for all the recruits in 1084 to watch and learn from. My screams and the yells from the Drill Instructor echoed deep into the eardrums of every Recruit in that squad bay. The importance of this lesson still echoes in my eardrums to this very day.

I have harnessed this same intensity in correcting men of my own. I have nearly lost it, when correcting soldiers at the range or while deployed. Fellow colleagues are surprised when they hear me yell in this manner; they always remark that it does not sound like me. Now as I write, I have to admit that perhaps it is, in fact, not me.

HIDDEN RAGE

Parris Island is truly a honeycomb of rage, violence, and chaos. It is the honey produced from all the efforts demanded in the efforts of warfare. This rage becomes you. It begins to possess you like a demon attempting to take your soul. The difference on the Island, is that this rage beast does not merely attempt. Rather, it succeeds.

Initially in the Marines and especially at Parris Island, one may not notice it. You may notice it in the same way a wolf may not realize the smell of blood while he is in the presence of his pack. The scent of blood may not be obvious until he is away from his pack.

I have noticed it several times. I only dabble in this rage on occasion. It is a very dangerous emotion to unleash. Once unleashed, it consumes everything that you are. This anger ignites everything around you and sets your soul aflame.

WEAPON CONDITIONS

Weapons Training Battalion has the potential to be one of the most dangerous places on Earth. It is a place where raw recruits are trained to be professional killers and then are given live ammunition. However, the Marines implement controls to mitigate the chaos. The military without order can be a very dangerous place.

The Marines taught four weapons conditions.

Condition 1: Magazine inserted, round in chamber, bolt forward, safety on, ejection port cover closed.
Condition 2: Not applicable to the M16A2 rifle.
Condition 3: Magazine inserted, chamber empty, bolt forward, safety on, ejection port cover closed.
Condition 4: Magazine removed, chamber empty, bolt forward, safety on, ejection port cover closed.

The recruits howled these new terms in rhythmic repetition, until these pieces of knowledge became mental memory. We repeated these threads of knowledge until one can call upon them as easily as one raises his hand. There is no question in the knowledge a recruit learns while at Parris Island. Learning things such as weapon conditions helps a Marine to become one with his weapon. You become the rifle and the rifle becomes you.

IMMEDIATE AND REMEDIAL ACTION

M16A2 rifles are dependable rifles and will typically fire in ideal conditions. Unfortunately, the dance floor of combat rarely takes place under ideal conditions. These rifles, like all weapon systems, will malfunction from time to time. Marine recruits are taught to quickly correct the malfunction and put their weapons back into action and send flesh-ripping bullets downrange toward their enemies.

I was first taught what is called "immediate action." These are the actions that a Marine was to perform quite literally to get his weapon back to into action. I was taught to conduct Tap, Rack, Bang.

Tap: Slap the bottom of the magazine
Rack: Pull the charging handle to the rear and release it
Bang: Sight and attempt to fire

This simple method is useful in correcting the majority of stoppages that may occur while employing the rifle. If the rifle still did not fire, we then employed remedial action with the handy acronym called "SPORTS."

S: Seek cover
P: Pull the charging handle to the rear and attempt to lock the bolt to the rear
O: Observe for a round or brass to be ejected and take appropriate action to clear the stoppage
R: Release the bolt
T: Tap the forward assist
S: Sight and attempt to fire

Applying SPORTS does take one out of the fight for a few moments. However, it corrects most problems short of a severe stoppage such as an exploding round.

SIGHT ALIGNMENT AND SIGHT PICTURE

Shortly after arriving to Weapons Training Battalion, Platoon 1084 was introduced to its PMI, Primary Marksmanship Instructor. My platoon was marched out to the range and stopped at an unoccupied range. It was now late August and the sun danced beautifully down upon the green field. I loved the sound of us marching on the open grass. Our sharp movements were nullified on the grass and the sound was truly a contrast to the normal sharp thuds we produced on concrete.

I smiled, only subtly to myself, as we marched at sling arms on the soft grass. I imagined we were colonial infantrymen marching on some cross-field advance to meet the British in battle on some lovely green. The scene seemed almost too perfect and I was happy.

The rifle range reiterated the Spartan approach that the Marines have to everything. The classroom came in sight. It looked like an old, neglected garage whose sidewalls had been torn down along ago. As 1084 closed the distance, a series of charts and a chalkboard became visible. The Drill Instructors continued to march and soon 1084 arrived under this archaic structure. 1084 waited and the Drill Instructor pulled back their reins.

The stress and methods of chaos utilized by the Drill Instructors are slackened somewhat while on the training grounds of the rifle range. This is not to say that one's time spent at the range is a stress-free environment. However, with live rounds inserted into the equation, it was unwise to push the stress envelope during initial training.

The PMI was then introduced. He was a large man, whose tanned cheekbones and hands told of numerous hours spent under the hot oppressive sun. His look was more normal as a regular looking Marine than the Drill Instructors. DIs are typically shredded men, because of the operational tempo of boot camp and the high demands of cardio vascular fitness necessary to be successful during training.

His face was warm and welcoming. He looked as if he could have been a high school football coach and his opening lines set us at ease.

"Alright, listen up. I am not a Drill Instructor. Do I even look like a Drill Instructor? No. My job is to teach you to shoot like Marines. When I am done with you, I promise you will be able to hit a man-sized target at 500 meters."

His speech placed all the nervous recruits at ease somewhat. I could both sense and see the distain in the DI's faces as they watched the PMI address us in a pleasant tone. I appreciated the short break from the chaos. However, the DIs ensured 1084 would be reminded where they were later that evening.

SIGHT ALIGNMENT AND SIGHT PICTURE

The Marines treat shooting with the amount of care and attention to detail the Catholic Church gives to preparing the Eucharist for holy communion. Sight alignment and sight picture are perhaps some of the most important fundamentals of marksmanship regardless of what type of weapon one may be employing. Without utilizing these important tenets, one cannot hope to hit a man-sized target at ranges beyond 100 meters.

Sight alignment refers to keeping the front sight post centered both vertically and horizontally in the rear sight aperture. Correct sight picture refers to placing the tip of the front sight post in the center of the target while maintaining correct sight alignment.

BREATH CONTROL

Some seem to think that since rifles made their appearance on the modern battlefield, the level of skill needed by a warrior has dramatically lowered. Granted it does not take a large amount of energy to point a weapon in a general direction and pull a trigger. However, to land accurate rounds at ranges of 300 meters or greater requires training, discipline, and skill.

Breathing is simply a part of being alive. A true warrior molds his life force around effectively delivering his strike of choice. It's a truth that all wrestlers, boxers, and all athletes know. Delivering an accurate round down range holds the same truth. I would argue that it is even more so important in shooting a rifle. This is critical, as the bullet becomes an extension of a shooter's body. This strike must be given at the crucial moment to land your breath of death upon the enemy.

Many laymen shooters have been taught from a young age to hold one's breath prior to sending a round downrange. This may seem to hold true for a good many of successful hunters in the woodlands and farmlands of the United States. However, skilled riflemen will need more than a few tricks to kill at ranges of over 300 meters.

Marines teach to make a shot by extending the natural respiratory pause. In a normal breathing cycle, there is a pause between taking your next breath. I was taught to pull the trigger during this pause. Skilled marksmen integrate breathing with the rest of the fundamentals of marksmanship.

TRIGGER CONTROL

As a layman shooter, I never put a great deal of thought into my trigger squeeze prior to boot camp. I simply acquired my target, and pulled the trigger. In any martial art, it is the smallest detail that can make the difference between victory or defeat. This martial truth holds well in the art of shooting as well.

Improperly pulling the trigger can dramatically throw the strike of the round off its intended target. I was trained in two methods of trigger control: uninterrupted and interrupted trigger control. In uninterrupted trigger control, one simply pulls out the initial slack of the trigger and finishes the pull in one smooth motion. Interrupted trigger control again reemphasizes taking out the initial slack of the trigger. However, one pauses if you lose you correct sight picture. You simply continue your trigger pull once you reacquire the proper sight picture.

BONE SUPPORT, MUSCULAR RELAXATION, AND NATURAL POINT OF AIM

The past few pages may have revolutionized how you may have looked at shooting. To Marines, all the fundamentals are designed to make you into an unshakable tripod capable of delivering 5.56mm rounds consistently on a man-sized target at 500 meters.

In each position, a Marine will attempt to maximize bone support and muscular relaxation. Anyone who has stared behind the sights of a rifle or pistol from a standing unsupported position, can undoubtedly tell you about their frustration in acquiring a good sight picture on their target. Granted, firing from a standing unsupported position is at times inevitable. However, extending one's limbs with a weighted object is a sure way to cause a bit of shaking. While this physical phenomenon is completely normal, it will almost certainly throw off the strike of your round.

Ensuring your body is maximizing bone support and muscular relaxation will ensure you have the conditions in place to achieve your natural point of aim.

The natural point of aim is one of the essential elements of marksmanship. Once in the position of your choice, you sight into your target. When the desired sight picture is acquired, you close your eyes, take a breath, and open your eyes. Almost always, the sight picture will be off. An unskilled shooter will move his arms to align his sight. Doing this, however, will break the tenet of muscular relaxation and cause your arms to eventually shake. Correcting the natural point of aim in this manner is often described as "muscling" it.

I was taught not to correct the sight picture by moving my arms. Rather, I was trained to correct my body position, thereby making the following shots more accurate. I was trained to correct the entire tripod, rather than merely correcting a small inefficiency.

SHOOTING POSITIONS AND SNAPPING IN

I honestly had no idea prior to my first classes of marksmanship on the island, that shooting could be such a complicated matter. My perspective regarding shooting was completely shattered and remodeled. The Marines wasted no time at all and soon moved on to the four basic shooting positions we would need to use to qualify on the Island: standing, kneeling, sitting, and prone.

The technicalities of any martial art contain a great deal of attention to detail to properly perform a technique. One may compare learning to shoot effectively as complicated as perhaps learning the basic elements of chess. We spent several hours each day learning and reinforcing the fundamentals of marksmanship.

I spent hours training the static prescribed shooting positions. I practiced the art form to the controlled commands from the Drill Instructors. It was years later where I found out that firing my rifle in battle was a dramatically different experience than the chess with a series of fixed positions in training. Instead, in the chaos of combat—shooting was like playing chess after doing six shots of Jack Daniels, while listening to "Master of Puppets" by Metallica.

SLINGS

Precision marksmanship is taken to the next level on Parris Island. I was trained to utilize different slings to assist in making accurate shots downrange. A well-placed sling can tighten shot groups at far distances. The two types of slings were called the hasty sling and the loop sling. The cloth tightly wrapped around my arm added lethality to my shooting.

SNAPPING IN BARRELS

I have found that the practice of snapping in is unique to the United States Marine Corps. The objective during this exercise is for a recruit to practice attaining proper sight picture/alignment and shooting positions on the painted silhouettes of the dog, able, and B-Mod targets. The practice takes hours of concentration; it was my holy warrior meditation.

At a glance, this practice may not seem entirely practical. However, it is one practice that assists Marine recruits to find comfort and precision within their shooting positions.

A LOOK INTO SNAPPING IN

My loop sling is tightly wrapped around my upper tricep. It is so tight that the flesh on my right shoulder is throbbing. I lie in the prone and sight in on the silhouette of my prey: a human. I switch my selector lever from safe to fire and I am ready to become Death. I close my eyes and take a breath. I stare into the darkness, because my eyelids have halted the sunlight from entering my gaze. I take a couple more deep breaths.

In this darkness, I am at peace. I only dare close my eyes for but a few seconds, but here I rest. I am the samurai here and focus, shutting out all otherworldly desires. I think not of girls, of home, food, nor of freedom. There is only the kill. The kill is what I must focus on. There is only one truth for a warrior. It is the truth of battle, an experience I did not find for years to come. However, as that young Marine recruit I didn't know that. The Marines taught us to be ready for a war that could erupt at any moment. We are kept hungry like starving wolves that bloodlust for a kill. We wait for the moment. Until then, we sharpen our fangs for the time when we first meet our prey.

Here, while I am alone for these few seconds, I imagine what it must be like to see my prey for the first time. I want it so bad that I can taste it. My meditation ends and I open my eyelids, allowing the sunlight to cascade down upon my eyes and revealing the world to me.

My eyes focus with the light and I stare at my front sight post on my rifle. The target appears fuzzy beyond it. However, there is a problem; my sight picture is off. The target waves in the heat of the air to the right of my front sight post. I will fix this problem, as I must destroy my enemy, who for the time being is that target in the distance. He is but a small silhouette target, only a few inches in length. He is only a black figure painted on the side of this white oil drum. However, at the moment, he is my mortal enemy. He is the bringer of death to all those that I love and my way of life. He wants to end me and tear my body and the body of mates into shreds. I will not allow him. I will fuck him up. I will spill his blood unto this grass before he can do the same to me. He is mine and I will conquer him. I am the guardian of all that is sacred in my world.

I will not muscle my sight onto him. I remember my training. I must ensure my sight is on my natural point of aim. I adjust my legs and move my body pointed toward him. I have acquired my target. But I am not done. I must return to the darkness again, to ensure I have acquired my sight. I close my eyes again and search for my warrior truth in the darkness. I take a deep breath in and I can taste the grass that I am lying on. It ignites a great slew of memories from youth on those football fields of Allen Park, Michigan. A multitude of boyhood memories cascade in front of me. However, it lasts for but a moment and I return to the predator that I am fast becoming. My breath is complete and I open my eyes.

Sunlight ignites my retina and sends wonderful images to my brain. I see what marksmen have prayed for since the invention of firearms. My sight picture and sight alignment is perfect. My target remains fuzzy in the background, as my front sight post cuts him in half. I am ready for the kill.

My breathing cycle continues and the respiratory pause places my front sight post exactly where I want and need it to be. I begin my BRASF(breathe, relax, sight, squeeze, fire, follow through). I am on my final approach to making my perfect kill. I breathe in the South Carolina air deeply, filling my lungs and watch as my front sight predictably raises over my target. The air begins to slowly release out of my lungs and I relax. Joyfully, my front sight post begins to fall lower and to where I need it to be to send an accurate round downrange. I aim and my sight is dead on as the last of my breath drains from my lungs. I begin to squeeze ever so slowly, I have taken out the initial slack of the trigger, only a feather of force is needed to complete my trigger squeeze. My breath is gone from my lungs and my sight holds true. It is time to the do the deed that I am designed and trained to do. It is time to bring death unto him. I pull my trigger.

I pull and hear the reassuring click of the firing pin. Had there been a live round in my chamber; I would have sent a round slamming directly into the body of my enemy, slaughtering the pig from the face of the earth. I follow through on my shot and release my trigger. The shot is complete.

Shooting to the Marines is the basis of who they are. Marines believe that they are the best marksmen on the face of the earth. It does not matter whether that is true. What does matter is that Marines believe that to be the truth. This confidence bleeds through all Marines, both officers and enlisted; at all ranks. It is this Marine cockiness that all young women near Marine bases fall victim to; at least once in their lives.

SHOOTING MEDITATION, AUDITORY EXCLUSION

Those who have tasted the strong wine of battle are all familiar with that moment in contact where all sound, time, and the world ceases to exist. It is this auditory exclusion which comes about in this time of high stress. I felt this in battle, years after Parris Island in Kunar Province. However, when I tasted battle, it was a familiar flavor. I sampled it before on those horribly hot days on the island.

The hyper focus placed upon the snapping in barrels and later at the known distance range can only be replicated within the perils of combat. There is no better meditation. For that brief moment in time, the only thing that exists is you, your rifle, and your target. Here behind the sights of a rifle is where a Marine belongs. This is his home to us who have worn the Eagle Globe and Anchor.

DATABOOK

Marine Corps marksmanship is as complex as it is devastatingly simple. I was trained in the use of the data book to help record and make adjustments to my sights. This is known as "dope" in the shooting world. Marine recruits are able to effectively place well aimed shots at 500 meters. This would be impossible, without making wind adjustments to the M16 A2.

These data books turn the relatively simple task of aiming and shooting into a highly complex affair of getting rounds on target. Even when winds are at 20 mph, I could place rounds on target at 300 meters. Prior to Boot Camp, my understanding of marksmanship was comparable to a third graders comprehension of multiplication tables. The Marines changed all of that. Armed with these new techniques, my understanding of shooting became like attempting to do calculus on the training field.

Grass week was fast coming to an end and the rifle became my world. My hours and days blended together on the training field. The Drill Instructors, along with the marksmanship Instructors, tirelessly corrected shooting positions, techniques, and breathing. I held the rifle so tight to my right shoulder that I had an abrasion on the pocket of my shoulder. Many of the recruits had these self-imposed wounds that are fondly called rifle strawberries.

Each week my company commander conducted a health inspection of the recruits under his command. It was another safety check implemented in this chaos of this Spartanesque training. 1084 stood online, following the morning PT shower, only wearing a towel and shower shoes. When the company commander approached a recruit, they turned around while flipping their hands upside down and stated the scripted line:

"Good morning, sir, this recruit has not physical or psychological problems to report at this time."

This was one weekly check Marine Corps officers conducted to ensure recruits were not injured, abused, or attempting to hide any injuries.

My CO noticed the abrasion on my shoulder and asked what it was. I proudly answered that it was from my snapping in drills. The Drill Instructor next to the commander let a small prideful smile crack from his lips. It was time to soon move to the firing range.

INITIAL PFT

Grass week was over, however the tests continued to challenge 1084. At this point of boot camp, several qualifying events continually came my way. The next major obstacle guarding the coveted Eagle Globe and Anchor was the Initial PFT (physical fitness test).

My conditioning, endurance, and stamina were top notched. The majority of recruits had cut anywhere from 10-30 lbs of body weight. My agility, strength, and endurance were at some of the highest levels of my entire life.

I breezed through the pull-ups and crunches portion of the PFT. The striking thing about this PFT was not the test itself. Rather, the PFT was conducted next to a military housing sector of the base. 1084 formed for the run portion of the test around 8:00am; school time for children.

It felt strange to be this close to what looked like normal civilian life. I watched several young mothers bring their school children to their respective bus stops. I permitted a small smile to crack through my face. The small school kids carried there brightly colored lunch boxes and played with one another without the slightest care in the world.

Seeing the mothers and the children was like seeing white doves fly on a battle field. They were beautifully innocent creatures and reminded me of the peaceful land that existed far from this land of orders, rage, and chaos. It was truly a breath of fresh air to see that the world still existed while I was living in this Sparta. It made all my efforts worth it.

The run was no challenge at all. Passing the PFT brought me one step closer to completing this hellacious journey of manhood. I looked forward to completing the rifle range. The rifle range was one of the final major steps to finishing Marine Corps Training. 1084 yearned to complete this portion of training.

RANGE WEEK

Platoon 1084 marched to the live fire rifle range. The very act of making it this far in training was a right of passage in itself. Now, the recruits were going to be trusted with live ammunition. 1084 marched up and formed in their firing orders in front of the towers. I was in the hands of the PMI and marksmanship Instructors. The Range safety personnel inspected the rifles onto the range, ensuring that none of the recruits had a stoppage in their barrels that would cause either a misfire or an injury to those on the firing line. The firing orders were separated; half went to the firing line and the others, with myself included, marched to the target pits.

TARGET PITS

The rifle ranges on Parris Island are known distance (KD) ranges. Recruits shoot their rifles and attempt to bring targets down from the 200, 300, and 500-yard line. The target pits lie behind a small earth berm encased in reinforced concrete and resembled a trench line, reminiscent of World War I. Targets are presented and hidden from the shooters view by an ingenious but archaic conveyor system. The targets themselves are made by recruits and housed in a small target shack.

Once reaching the pits, the recruits were assigned to different targets and some of are sent to the target factory. The men in my relay were sent to target #4. Before the firing began, we were given a short class on how to run the target pits.

All commands on the rifle range were given from the tower, whose voice had total control over every Marine and recruit on the range. On the command "TARGETS" I raised my target in the air, by dropping the counter weight on the conveyor system. I watched and listened for the shots. It was there where I learned to recognize what a bullet sounds like when it breaks the air overhead.

The crack of an incoming bullet flying over your head is unmistakable. A bullet can pass a few meters to your right or left and you will hear still it. However, the shock and indication of an overhead shot is much different. The air breaks over your head like a "WHIP-SNAP." It sounds like nothing else on earth. It sounds like Death. I have only heard this sound in two places in my life. The first was in the target pits of a known distance range and the second was in the heart of a firefight with an enemy who was trying to kill me.

This horrid sound can cause different reactions, depending on where it is one happens to encounter it. There, in the pits, it meant that the bullet impacted the target and a recruit had to lower it to mark the bullet's impact. I lowered the target and diligently searched for the small bullet hole produced by the 5.56mm round. Once the hole was identified, I placed a small spindle, either black or white, circle on where bullet landed on the target, marking its position. Once marked, the target was raised back into the shooters field of view. Should a shooter miss his target, the recruits in the pit, raise a lollipop-like marker and wave it across the target's mast.

I enjoyed my time working in the target pits. It was laid back, except that small dreadful feeling in my stomach that somehow I might not qualify. Speed was critical in the pits, as the faster the target service, the more time was allotted to the shooter during the slow fire portions of the range.

Time in the pits was a welcomed break and I made small talk with the other recruits. My time on the island was becoming a normal way of life and I felt very close to the men around me. My mates and I shared some of the most traumatic experiences one can have outside the battlefield. We sat next to each other and listened to the horrible orchestra of shock, violence, and anger in the form of bullets going overhead.

The shooting began with the 300 meter zero. Bullets cracked and whistled overhead. Sounds such as these became familiar and later became more useful on battlefields far from this island. My mates and I on target 7 and relay 4, worked as speedily as possible marking the targets for the shooters down range. Slower pit crews were ridiculed by the Drill Instructors in the target pits. The range tower provided less subtle corrections by sounding sarcastically motivated words of encouragement such as:

"Let's go target 5…. Some time before his ETS (end of the Marine's enlistment)."

The heat of the day steadily increased in the pits as the recruits continued their prescribed shooting on the range.

At midday, C company broke for chow and I was acquainted with another essential portion of Marine Corps culture: "the bag nasty." This meal was essentially a sandwich, chips, a drink, and an apple wrapped in brown lunch sack, which reminded me of my elementary school lunches. The hunger that tugged at my belly was a constant reminder of the sheer amount of calories I burned on those training fields. That day on particular, I ate the entire apple, including the core, with the exception of the apple stem. I ate quickly, as I always did, and prepared myself to move to the firing line.

"Cease fire! Cease fire! Cease fire!" boomed over the speakers.

Half of 1084 formed up in ranks and marched to the 300m line. Following an additional safety brief, I moved to my assigned target lane. My eyes caught an object which seemed to add a great deal of mystique to the rifle range: "Smudge pots." Smudge pots were small black pots with a burning flame atop them. I marched up to the flame and placed my front sight post into the fire. The fire blackened the sight and made attaining proper sight picture a bit easier. It seemed a bit too fitting to place one's spear into the fire before presenting yourself on the battlefield to Mars and his servants. After completing my battlefield field zero at 300 meters, I moved up to the 200-meter line to commence the Marine Corps known distance qualification table.

This known distance table was called Table 1. Table 1 firing consisted of shooting in both slow and rapid-fire scenarios. I watched with a great deal of anticipation as the first of the shooters took aim and began their string of fire. The wind was less than five mph, as told by the near lack of movement in the range flag. I looked at my data book and took note of the adjustment, should I have to adjust my sights if the wind picked up.

It was my turn.

My heart rate picked up somewhat in anticipation for the upcoming action. My coach, CPL Ski, handed me my ammunition. I loaded three magazines of five rounds each, and one magazine of ten rounds. Listening to the tower, I took my seat in the cross-legged fashion that I was instructed to perform. Next, I adjusted my loop sling with its predetermined length for sitting from grass week, upon my tricep. My elbows were locked within the inside pockets of my knee. The pits raised the portable bulls-eye targets and I sighted in. My eyes closed and I achieved that small Zen moment as I established my natural point of aim on that black circle downrange. I opened my eyes and received some good fortune, as I was dead on. I waited for my call to battle.

"Load!" The tower ordered.

I slammed one magazine of five rounds into my rifle and re-established my point of aim. I waited.

"Make ready!" The tower ordered.

I pulled the charging handle back to the rear and released it. I conducted a hasty brass check, to ensure that a round was properly chambered. I ever so slightly pulled back on the charging handle and observed the shiny brass of the 5.56mm properly seated. I chambered death. With a smile, I returned the charging handle, closed my ejection port cover, and tapped the forward assist. My weapon was now on condition 1 and I was ready.

The rifle becomes an utterly different object when you have a round chambered in it. You inject a life taking serum into this rifle and it becomes a beast. It stands ready to do your bidding. You instantly become that Grim Reaper you have only heard about in your nightmares. You become more than human and more than death. You become evil and a hunter of men. You can harvest any that may come your way. You are ready.

It would be over a decade from that moment to when I locked and loaded on a combat patrol. I did this sacred act thousands of miles away—over seas, continents, deserts, and mountains. I later conducted this act in a small ancient valley called the Watapor, in Afghanistan. I would be an officer and leader of men then. However, I will never forget the first day that I locked and loaded my M16 A2 service rifle on that hot summer day on Parris Island.

"Shooters, at this time move your selector switch from safe

to fire and engage your targets when they appear." The tower ordered.

My selector switch made that click that instantly gave me the power to rob men of their souls. It is a sound that all veterans and especially combat veterans are intimately familiar with. It is the signal for the harvest to begin.

The half second it took for the targets to peer over the berm felt like an eternity. I took a few deep breaths in an effort to quell my heart rate's anticipation for the upcoming shot. Slowly, the targets rose, jiggled for an instant, and then came to rest.

My target is still; and I must end it.

I closed my eyes, returning to the cool darkness, and breathed ever so deeply. My breath was gone and my eyes opened. My aim was off ever so slightly and I adjusted my legs a few centimeters. I shut my eyes and breathed deeply again. My eyelids opened and I was dead on.

"Breathe, relax, aim, squeeze…. Bang! and follow through." I silently chanted to myself.

The target fell.

I peered down at my data book and called (call = guess where your shot will land based on your last aiming point prior to shooting) my shot with a dot in the dead center of the target. My assessment of the shot was verified by the white disk smack dead center of the target. I plotted my hit with a number 1 in the data book. I finished the remainder of my magazine in the seated position.

A warrior learns to appreciate the many benefits of laying close to the earth when he begins his education into the art of war. In addition to providing cover from the enemy's munitions; there are few better platforms that provide a more stable shooting platform. The further a warrior moves his body away from using the earth as support, the more the weapon wobbles off target.

I unloaded my weapon and moved into my kneeling position. I adjusted the sling with a bit more slack and locked/loaded my next five round magazine. The target was already up. I sighted in and began my pseudo meditative shooting cycle drilled into me from the hours of snapping in drills during grass week. The rounds flew from my rifle and I recorded their deadly progress in my data book, my diary of death.

It was not I who fired the rifle. It was the Marine Corp's energy that flew through my soul without a prompt. I was on auto pilot and allowed the created predator within me to search for the kill. I thought of nothing else in that moment. There was only the target and me.

I will bring him down before he has the same chance to bring me down. It will be me that goes home following this engagement. My family and friends will welcome me home with hugs and kisses. My enemy will have a different fate.

I will ensure he goes home in a box, wrapped in the colors of his homeland. I will send this death in the form of 5.56mm spiraling into his body. I will shred his internal organs and make him bleed, both inside and outside of his body. His breath will drain out of his vessel and leave me in peace.

The target and I square off, as if he is my sacred enemy. He and I will square up, like the dozens of times on the field of battle years later in my life.

The shots continued and my five round magazines fired off their payload of death. I placed my weapon on safe, pressed my magazine ejector, and dropped my mag. I was nearly finished with the slow-fire portion at the 200-yard line. I stood up.

My final five rounds in the slow fire were expended in the standing position. I unhooked my loop sling that was tightly coiled around my right tricep and reconnected it to the rifle;

slightly inverted. I straightened my left arm through and wrapped it around my arm in a hasty sling. I locked/loaded and peered through my sights.

While standing, one realizes the extreme importance the earth has in supporting a shooting position. My front sight post performed a slow gradual swim around the target. Shooting in this position is not nearly as precise and it was essential to take all the slack out of the trigger, especially here. I squeezed the moment my sights found refuge within the proper sight picture. I fired, called, and plotted. The five rounds were complete.

The Marine rifle coaches acted as fathers while on the range. They acted as the recruit's beloved assistant gunners, aiding to get rounds on target. I had complete confidence in this CPL, whose faded cammies and chiseled body told of an unforgiving life in the Fleet Marine Force, or what is commonly referred to as the "Fleet." He carefully and patiently told me calming helpful words such as "quit breathing or watch your trigger control."

I prepared myself for the first rapid fire on the qualification table. I locked and loaded a 10-round magazine and waited for the signal to take the sitting position.

"Targets!" Echoed from the range tower and I swiftly dropped into the sitting position. I had a total of 60 seconds to unload my magazine downrange. Within a second of hitting the ground; the entire line of recruits erupted into a beautiful cacophonic orchestra of death downrange. I had no idea at the time that this sound aided to indoctrinate a Marine for the firefights he may encounter years later in some godforsaken city or valley.

I pulled my trigger, slowly and carefully each time. Each shot delivered downrange was a precision guided piece of lead sent toward my enemy. I was complete.

I picked up with the entire line and walked back to the

300-meter line. I adjusted my elevation and took notice of the wind. I was careful to ensure that I had the proper "dope" in the weapon. Ammunition was issued, one five round magazine and one ten round magazine.

I assumed my kneeling position and my tight loop sling around my tricep. With a magazine of five rounds I locked and loaded. It is a particular hard thing to keep your heart rate low when you lock and load. There is no fooling the body for what is about to happen. Although heightened a bit under the shadow of contact, locking and loading will excite the primal self on any military rifle range.

You can't fool yourself when you lock and load a round into your chamber. The primal predator buried deep within you becomes awake. You might as well pick up your leash in front of your dog and pretend like you are not taking a walk. The primal hunter is conscious now and it demands a kill. It happens each and every time. You get as excited as a young man seeing a beautiful model wrapped in the most seductive lingerie possible. His body will know exactly what to do without a prompt. It is the same thing when you ready your body for action on either the range or the field of battle. There is no lying to yourself or about the mortal activity you are about to indulge in.

The five rounds were fired without incident. I did well and I prepared for the rapid fire — from standing to prone. I adjusted my sling to its pre-marked position for the prone and awaited my order.

"Lock and load! and "Make Ready!"

It was time to go again.

I dropped into the prone and sighted in. I learned to love the prone as it gave me the ability to slice down my targets at will. The ten seconds unfolded before my eyes and ears in the special beauty that battle keeps for her warriors. The firing was complete. We picked up and moved out to the 500m line.

500 METER LINE

Perhaps one of the greatest gifts the Marines pass on to their recruits is confidence in long-range marksmanship. Marines, regardless of gender, have the ability to take life at 500 meters without the help of an optic. The ability to take out an enemy at over a quarter mile is a gift, I forever cherish.

I felt doubt when I first heard about taking out a target at 500 meters without a scope.

I laid down at the 500-meter line with my loop sling tightly gripping my tricep. I already was locked and loaded. I sighted in. The intimidating thing about the 500-meter line is that a front sight post can completely cover the entire B-Mod target. A shooter has to lower the front sight post in aiming to reveal the silhouette in the distance.

A Marine in a solid prone position, complimented by a tight loop sling on good ground, is a nearly perfect weapon system. Providing the wind is not too crazy, most Marines can rein havoc down upon 500-meter targets.

I was given clearance to fire and set in. My selector switch moved from safe to semi. After a few breaths, I found my natural point of aim. I was ready. I squeezed ever so slowly and waited for all my breath to leave my lungs. The breath was gone and my aim was ready. I squeezed off a round. I called it dead center and waited. When the target appeared, the large white spindle plotted my shot just below my target's shoulders.

202 | ANTONIO M. SALINAS

"Holy fuck." I said under my breath.

I was amazed that I was able to hit targets at such a range. I had never tried a shot over 200 meters in my life, let alone 500 meters, before coming to Parris Island.

Range week continued and each day my shooting abilities held true. I knocked down target after target. Shooting became just a bit too easy. I took well to these disciplined positions. 1084 continued with the same shooting all week from Monday—Thursday. I was not concerned about qualifying, and arrogantly I thought I would qualify without a hitch.

However, for some reason, the stress of qualification day got to me. Although my shooting thus far ensured that I was going to qualify, I heard horror stories about other recruits not being able to qualify and having to be recycled.

Fear is one of the greatest enemies a warrior can have. It can have devastating effects on the mind of a warrior and tear his confidence into shreds. Fear can spread through one's blood like a cancer. Like water freezing into stone, it can rip apart the strongest mountains of man, until you are little more than shale. It is okay to feel fear, we all do. However, it must be controlled or it will destroy you.

OVER CONFIDENCE, FEAR, AND HUMBLING LESSONS

I heard rumors in the target pits on pre-qualification day regarding a few recruits who failed to qualify and were forced to recycle. The thing about rumors is that they tend to mutate the longer they are in existence. I heard even more horrible rumors regarding recruits that failed to qualify at all and were sent home without the title of Marine.

The longer one is on the island earning the title Marine is comparable with staying alive. This title; this perpetual source of pain, struggle, noise, and violence was my reason to exist. Becoming a Marine was all that mattered to me. I wanted the Eagle, Globe, and Anchor above anything else in life. At this point of the training; success went well beyond patriotism, a promise of an adventure, or money for college. Rather, this journey was fueled by pure personal ambition. This journey became me. I was in hell and my time in the flames would not fade away to the pages of history.

As qualification day came closer, fear spread throughout my soul. There were a couple of recruits who had recycled and joined the platoon. The Marines give you an additional week to qualify; should you fail to qualify. I looked at the few recruits who were recycled into my platoon. These men were near broken and their fear of failure spread to me.

On the eve of the qualification, my nerves were on fire and burned every inch of me. I had succumbed to this sickness called fear. A warrior's world is composed of completing tasks on the cusp of death in the shadow of fear. Fear is the world for warriors. It is present in what we must do in battle. It must be mastered by those who practice war. On this night, I failed to do so.

I desperately tried to sleep. However, the fear fermented in my veins. I woke up that night in a cold sweat and felt sick to my stomach. I felt the bile working its way up my digestive track. Quickly, I slid on my shower shoes and ran to the head.

I ran directly toward the nearest toilet and bent over the bowl. My nerves were expelled out of my mouth within my vomit. I distinctly watched as the green beans from my dinner were thrown into the toilet. I stood there with my mouth wide as the heaves began to erupt from my mouth with those pitiful moans reminiscent of having one too many drinks the night before.

The recruit on fire watch approached me and asked if I was okay. I nodded and walked to the sink to wash up. After cleansing myself, I stared into the mirror with my bloodshot eyes with an innate look of misery. It was a look that I rarely saw in my eyes. It was defeat.

I defeated myself before the first round left my barrel on qualification day. I allowed the fear to enter my mind and then my bloodstream. It was a lesson that I would not forget throughout the annals of my military career. It would not be the last time feeling fear. I felt it again before my first action years later in Kunar province.

Qualification day came, and like any other day blessed by Murphy, my lack of confidence was enhanced by unfavorable winds. The fear of defeat spread in me like venom from a bite. I could not find my Zen moment during my breathing cycle. My bullets found their mark on a few targets, but it was not good enough. At the end of the day, I shot a 175, just five points short of qualifying.

My heart fell into the lower depths of despair in my warrior soul. I thought I was done for. I was only a few points from qualifying. However, the title Marine then seemed to be an ocean away from me. I stared at the picture of my girlfriend that I kept in my data book. Tears welled up in my eyes at the thought of being away from her even longer. I also thought of the disgrace I would feel should I return to my homeland without this holy title.

1084 left Weapons battalion and moved back to the main side barracks. I did my best to swallow my fears and hold my sadness in check. However, my distress was obvious. I am typically a very positive happy man. So much so that even to this day anyone who knows me can instantly tell if I am sad. It was as obvious as a rain cloud appearing in the middle of a drought in the Mojave Desert.

Once unpacked in the barracks of 1084, the Drill Instructors fell us in on line. The congratulated us on qualifying. However, these beasts of men were not the bastards or the compassionless monsters that Hollywood makes them out to be. They knew how bad every man in the squad bay wanted to be a Marine. At this point in recruit training, the clear majority of the non-hackers had been weeded out. We all wanted to be Marines.

The Drill Instructor motivated those of us who were unqualified, or commonly referred to as UNQs. They stated:

"Ears!"

"Open Sir!"

"We are getting ready for Team week in the chow hall. However, this weekend we are going to help the recruits who UNQed on the range get ready to shoot on Monday! They will all qualify. Is that understood?"

"Sir, yes Sir!"

I was instantly emboldened. Marine Corps leadership is amongst the most draconian I have seen in my years of service. However, with that said, it is also the most caring in the military. Those few words uttered by the Drill Instructors were just enough to kindle a spark of hope in the dark cold winter of my heart. Marines have an ability to inspire courage by mere words. It is in the most helpless of moments that mere words can serve as guides through the darkness.

HOPE REKINDLED

That weekend I refined all my techniques. I was partnered up with a very skilled recruit that was an NRA national marksman. He went over my shooting positions with me and coached me through them. The soft, caring words of a comrade are very soothing and can keep one going during dark moments. His guidance provided confidence to my shooting positions and gave me the faith that I was desperately looking for.

That Sunday, church was especially more meaningful to me. It is sad that only in hard times that many search for God's light to get us through the journey. I used every spare moment to hone my positions.

When Monda, I was ready for the upcoming battle.

TEAM WEEK AND SECOND CHANCES

Team week began. A few recruits were sent on various details such as cutting grass or laundry. However, the clear majority of the platoon was sent to work the grueling hours inherent of all military chow halls.

It was different for the UNQs.

The unqualified shooters assembled outside the barracks and waited in the pre-dawn darkness. A Drill Instructor came out with a roster and called off the names. My name was called and I boarded the bus.

We were bused back out to weapons Battalion. We dismounted the bus and I looked to the sky as we waited for dawn. The constellation Orion was there and seemed to bless my battlefield there. I felt at ease, as the late summer cool breeze kissed my flesh. The sun finally rose and with it came remedial rifle coaching time.

These Marines were very skilled at teaching UNQs. The SSgt began his instruction by saying:

"How many of you thought you were going to fail, before qual day even started."

The clear majority of the recruits in attendance, including myself, raised their hands.

"That is your biggest mistake. The shooting positions work and your equipment is good. Trust yourselves, your equipment, and your training; and I promise that each and every one of you will qualify and become United States Marines with your platoons. How does that sound?"

We all answered with a triumphant, "Ooh Rah!"

Monday, was only a pre-qual day. We had the opportunity to qualify every day from that Tuesday-Friday. Those that could not would be recycled. The weather was perfect for shooting and my practice string of fire would have enabled me to score sharpshooter. My confidence was back and I was happy.

TUESDAY, OVERCONFIDENCE AND INTEGRITY.

I was ready. I was confident in my abilities, my training, and equipment. I could not fail nor would I. I walked as a new man; an angel of death on that battlefield. I knew I would slaughter my enemies on the range. I only had to show up and shoot. The targets would fall. I would give them no choice.

I was near flawless at the 200 and 300-meter line. I was dropping the targets at will and scoring very high. I knew I would be a sharpshooter (although if you qualify on this week, you are still a Marksman). However, there was something there that I did not know I was doing wrong.

I was overconfident.

As much as an enemy as fear is to warriors; overconfidence can have equally devastating effects. An over confident Marine or leader can lead his men into the jaws of death, but also somewhere where salvation can be impossible. This was the case for me.

I became so overconfident that I became arrogant on the 500-yard line. Arrogance can get you killed, or in this case, make you forget about the world that you exist in. I wanted to see my score as tallied by the recruit behind me, just behind the firing point. We were never told not to look at the scores, but such thing was not needed to be told. It was simply wrong.

I arrogantly walked to the recruit with my scorecard, without even bothering to see if any coaches or other Marines were watching. The score indicated that I had already qualified and my heart glowed with warm pride. The glory lasted for only a moment… when a Marine range safety NCO saw me.

"Hey, Recruit! What are you doing?"

I didn't even have time to respond.

"You were looking at your scorecard! Weren't you???! You can't friggin do that!"

My mind was swelling in despair and I answered with pitiful statements such as:

"Yes Sir! Aye, Aye Sir!"

More Marines moved in, and the harsh treatment continued. What's more is that I had just locked and loaded my 10-round magazine in my rifle. Perhaps the Marines wanted to test my reaction. I actually felt somewhat horrified to be in this mental state with a magazine in my rifle. My face was flushed and I fought to keep the tears in me.

One particularly large Marine joined in the feeding frenzy of yelling and looked at me.

"Oh.. so.. you want to be an integrity violator huh!? Good!" He took my scorecard and ripped it in half.

"Well guess what… you failed, Recruit! You will be here tomorrow, then the day after that and the day after that! You will be recycled and maybe never graduate! How does that sound!?"

He might as well have ripped my heart in half. My soul was on fire, and a few tears fell out of my eyes. I remained at the position of attention as the yelling continued. I knew I had to keep my bearing. I took the yelling and the pain.

I took it. I accepted the chaos. I became the chaos.

Something happened in all the hell ensued by the Marines screaming in my face. I found my Zen moment of peace. I did not ignore the chaos. Rather I simply accepted it. My mind became clear, which further infuriated the attacking Marines. I allowed the tears to clean the dust out of my eyes. The yelling finally stopped as it was my turn to shoot.

The young CPL who was my rifle coach felt bad for me. He did not join in the feeding frenzy. I lay down in my prone with my heart on fire and my mind somehow cooled. The CPL looked at me in the eyes and said:

"Just try to relax and fire. Everything will be okay."

His words emboldened me. I closed my eyes and shut the chaos of the world out around me. The Marines in the frenzy watched, expecting that I would fuck up.

I hit ten out of the ten targets in the black. It was best I had ever performed on the 500-meter line. I was confident that I could do it again.

I told a few of my friends about the ordeal on the bus back to the barracks. They reassured me not to worry and that I would just have to qualify the next day. I smiled and felt a bit better.

When we arrived back at the barracks, the Drill Instructors asked us how we did. SSgt Staley asked me and I told him that I had qualified, but was deemed an integrity violator. He grinned and told me to qualify tomorrow.

PEACE, UNEXPECTED

That was a tough night. However, I felt confident enough that I would qualify again. The next morning started just as before. The UNQs lined up on the bus and were transported to range. I dismounted and waited for roll call and the target relays to be assigned, when something unexpected occurred. My name was not called and I informed the Drill Instructor.

He asked if I had qualified. I told him the circumstances surrounding my range time on the previous day. I was told to stand by and I overhead him speaking to one of the range personnel. The range Marine told the Drill Instructor that the scorecard in the pits was all that mattered.

The Drill Instructor came to me and said some of the loveliest words I have heard from a Marine while at Parris Island, "You qualified recruit. Stand by for the range detail."

It was one of the happiest moments of my life. Tears of joy were welling within me, but I maintained my bearing. It was at that point that I knew I would become a United States Marine. Nothing would stop me. I was at peace.

The lesson of overconfidence was one of my most memorable lectures during my tenure at Parris Island.

That day was one of my most blissful days on the island. I spent it on the range conducting random details such as cleaning the range heads, or restocking toilet paper. I was marched to a different rifle range as well. There I was given a random experience to see something that I was not expected to see that closely for some time: girls and hundreds of them.

A few recruits and I were placed on the range for 4th Battalion training — all females. I thought, I was in heaven after qualifying and now I was lucky enough to see all these young women who were in prime condition. It was a treat that I thought too good to be true. However, I knew that the punishments of being caught staring at the females would be met with unforgiving ferocity. I did my best to make the best out of the day that an 18-year-old male could do in this environment.

I was moved to the target pits, still surrounded by hundreds of these women. I dared not to glare at them, but rather simply enjoyed hearing their comforting voices and catching glimpses of their heavenly bodies. I restrained my glaring smile from cracking too far out of my mouth. I was truly happy and took this great day for the gift that I knew it was.

LIGHT AT THE END OF THE TUNNEL

Over my first days of recruit training, SSgt Telford motivated us.

"If you want it, you will all leave Parris Island in 13 weeks as United States Marines. But I'm telling you recruits… you have to want it. Do you?"

" Sir, yes Sir!" 1084 replied.

"Can you see the end of the tunnel?" He asked.

Again, we answered:" Sir, yes sir!"

"No, you can't." He replied with that evil toned sarcasm that many Drill Instructors seem to be innately gifted with.

Today it was different. After qualifying on the rifle range I knew that I had a very strong chance of becoming a United States Marine. For the first time after arriving on Parris Island, I could actually see the light at the end of the tunnel. Hope was in sight.

1084 REUNION, TEAM WEEK

Near sunset, the shooters assembled back outside the buses scheduled to take us back to main side. My heart glowed with hope, power, and happiness. All the other recruits who had originally UNQed in my platoon had passed as well. You could feel the happiness in the air. All of us blew sighs of relief at this next accomplishment.

We pulled into 1st Battalion's area and were herded back to the barracks. SSgt Telford inquired at the scores and looked happy that we all had made it. The next morning, I joined my platoon in the Chow hall for the remainder of team week festivities.

That night was amongst my happiest while at Parris Island. My time at the Marine Corps rifle range provided me with a wide range of gifts in the science of warfare. I knew that I could repeatedly take a man's life at distances ranging from 200-500 meters. Regardless of the wind or weather conditions I knew that I could hurl lead over a quarter mile without the assistance of any scope or optic and spill my enemy's blood onto the dirt of the earth. I knew I could rob a man of the air that he breathed in his lungs.

Shooting and the Marine's training up to this point made me into this well toned and well-trained killing machine. I became what I had failed to overcome on the range. I became fear and learned of fear.

I will never forget the dreadful impact of fear on the fabric of a warrior. Fear can take a normally confident man and shred him into nothing. It can rip you open, spilling all your shortcomings into the ocean of doubt that you swim in. This fear is not only self destructive, but also a threat to those who share the waters around you. Fear can spread through the water like chum and it will bring about these Great White Sharks of death.

Fear circles you slowly at first. When you see this fear circling around you, it only increases your vulnerability. A warrior must try hard not to fall victim to such a horrid enemy.

I smiled with a huge grin as I lay in my bunk that night. I held the covers a bit tighter that evening. I took comfort under the heavy wool blanket whose itchiness was held at bay by a thin white sheet. I lay there at night, fantasizing about the many great adventures that I knew awaited me in the years ahead while in the legions of the Untied States Military.

TEAM WEEK

1084 awoke early for chow hall duty, around 0330 in the morning. The morning rising was still greeted with that loathsome amount of intensity as dressing for the day was still done by the numbers and would be for nearly the remainder of my time on

Parris island. The hour was early, even for us who were by used to waking up well before the first rays of light touched the earth.

Following the usual morning soaked in chaos, 1084 formed up outside the barracks. It was September, and the air was a tad cooler and crisper I noticed as I stared beyond the marshlands behind 1st Battalion. The morning dew and fog marked the change of season in the air.

My mates had been working in the chow hall for three days by the time I arrived from my remedial rifle training. 1084 still had two days left. Chow hall duty, as dull in comparison to something like pugil stick bouts or the rifle range, actually holds an important place in Marine Corps culture in the Fleet Marine Force.

The Marine Corps receives the least amount of funding in the defense budget as compared to the other services. Marines have always been expected to do more with less. This Spartanesque method of thinking carries on to all tenets of life in the Marine Corps, even in Marine Chow halls. Marine chow halls are run by qualified cooks who attend MOS (military occupational specialty) school to do their job. However, the horrid duty of serving and washing dishes is left to Marines who are sent on detail from their units. It is a horrible duty, but is necessary and saves the USMC millions of dollars each fiscal year.

1084 marched up and neatly filed into the chow hall. The atmosphere remained tense. However, the Drill Instructors relinquished a bit of their control by this point in the training cycle. This release was done for two reasons. First, because the nature of the job had spread the recruits out into a wide array of sections to keep the chow hall functioning, ranging from food prep, serving, back room cleaner, drink station, and tending to the head. The second reason was a fruit harvested by the harsh training for the past two months.

Discipline was the fruit of the Drill Instructor's efforts. This was not the discipline of doing the right thing under supervision. This was true discipline and the kind that keeps professional militaries functioning in the harshest of conditions. This discipline ensured that each recruit had the pride and honor to do the right thing, even when out of earshot of a Drill Instructor.

I, along with the remainder of the recruits, began doing what we would later do as Marine NCOs and for me as an officer. The recruits began taking care of their own and enforcing the hard fought standards so horribly earned here on the plains of Mars. It is this same type of discipline that forces effective combat units to clean their weapons, maintain their vehicles, and to constantly rehearse operations while on campaign in god-forsaken places such as Kunar or Helmand Province, Afghanistan. The most valuable lessons of discipline are those enforced by the men who live under their yoke.

REALITY

Team week also offered a glimmer of reality into the Marine Corps. Up to that point in their military journey, recruits were presented with Marine's who more or less represent the important tenets of a professional military presence. Prior to leaving for boot camp, Marine hopefuls met recruiters. Recruiters are in the mid point of their careers and must conduct their missions of recruiting Marine applicants as diligently as if they were conducing a route clearance mission on an IED strewn road in Iraq.

The professionalism displayed by the Drill Instructors goes without saying. Marine rifle cadre were very well trained, and the gravity of the task they taught was so important that they have little room to display anything less than exemplarily. The chow hall provided a picture into the reality and the non-ideal reality of the Marine Corps. We met Lance-Corporals.

The Lance Corporal is the third rank in the enlisted rating scheme. It is the final rank prior to making Corporal and becoming a leader of Marines; a non-commissioned officer. Some Marines may only have this rank for just over a year or so. Others, however, may wear this single chevron and crossed rifles for more than a few years. Marines not deemed worthy of leadership may in fact never see the rank of corporal.

The cooks had their NCOs watch over their Marines and recruits as well. These NCOs were as fit and professional as any. However, anyone who has served in the military will tell you that a good majority of first termers pray for the end of their enlistment each morning prior to coming to PT.

I saw it in these LCPLs. I remember one cook saying: "Have you ever been so tired, that you just can't bear to keep your eyes open?" I studied some of these young Marines with intrigue. Seeing the few unmotivated ones move about in the galley was a valuable lesson into the reality of Marines and of all military personnel in general. Veterans have all served with these type of men before. Some may have even been in charge of them. They have been in every military, regardless of iron discipline, since the time of Caesar.

Arriving late to team week, I was blessed with a stroke of luck with my position. My station was watching and cleaning the dining area. Recruit etiquette in the chow hall insured that messes, spills, and crumbs on the tables and floors were kept to a minimum. At this point of the training, I knew to take good details for exactly what they were: good fortune.

Team week taught me about the misery that military cooks must endure to complete their mission. I attained a large amount of respect for cooks during that brief experience into that world. I have served in a variety of capacities from intelligence, to infantry, and planning. I can tell you that my time spent working in a military chow hall have been amongst the most miserable times of my life. I would rather spend months patrolling a mountain side in Kunar, than a couple of weeks working in a chow hall.

All in all, team week was a lovely break in some respects from the horrors of the training that I had undergone thus far at Parris Island. The greatest element, which provided some relief, was the lack of control exuded by the Drill Instructors. The recruits of 1084 began to act like Marines, attacking the mission at hand and utilizing the attention to detail deeply bred within them.

The best thing about team week by far was the general proximity to graduation. Sure, there was a few more inspections and runs. However, the only real test that remained was the crucible. The final event known as the crucible existed only as legend in my mind. The crucible was like a storm brewing far off in the horizon. I was ready for this beast and I was eager to face her.

A-LINE

The majority of infantry training came later at MCT (Marine Combat Training) or for many Marines at SOI (School of Infantry). However, a few days were spent learning the elements of the Marine shock culture. A-Line focused on the elements of combat shooting.

Successful military commanders and fighters in any martial art know the truth that lies deeply hidden within the misty folds in the fog of war. Recruits snap in, march, and drill in the confines of a controlled environment. Here in the comforts of a parade field or a grassy rifle range recruits train both their minds and bodies in a deeply complicated ballet of movements necessary for exporting violence and taking the lives of the enemy. Recruits acquire, breathe, relax, aim, and squeeze. They listen for carefully calculated commands and triggers of attack. They are within a few feet of resupply, water, and medical assistance should any feel faint. However, at center of contact the reality of battle is much different. Words can never truly and completely bring to light the chaos felt in battle. Like a boxer performing his well rehearsed jab in a middle of a fight, warriors must perform or face conquest ourselves.

A-Line was an opportunity for recruits to employ the well rehearsed shooting positions in realistic shooting positions. I learned to fire from bunkers, around corners, and from simulated rooftops. I found it much more enjoyable to the rigidness of shooting on the green grasslands of rifle ranges. In addition to shooting, the platoon performed the maneuvers that prepared us for the violent movements of combat.

NIGHT INFILTRATION COURSE

1084 assembled on a late afternoon and was given a class on moving through the darkness in a wooded area. Enemy forces often guard their forward positions with booby traps, using piano wire like triggering devices. I was instructed how to utilize my hands to find these booby traps. In combat scenarios, these piano wires would emit a horrid explosion from a claymore or a mine. Here, on Parris Island the effects were only a night flare and recruits had to shout: "Recruit (insert name here), PLT 10??, I'm dead."

Night fell upon the Earth and my platoon halted at the entrance of a dark wood. Recruits conducted this exercise on their own in staggered starts. I waited on edge for my turn. To my front, it was quiet, like it always was prior to any action. Out of the silent night then emitted a glare from one of the triggered booby traps. I heard a recruit shout his instructed line in the forest and could detect the shame in that man's voice. I was determined not to be one of them.

My turn was up and an order to advance was given. I inched forward into the dark foreboding night. I used my left hand and moved it in an up to down fashion to feel for any traps. As I moved, I found a stick that was about four feet in length and decided to use this to scan for any threats. I held it in front of me in hopes that the stick would find any wires. It worked.

I found my first trap at about neck level. Although, it was only a simulated trap, the thought of being mangled by a real one displayed a collage of horrible pictures through my head. I dismissed it and began tracing the wire around to one of its flanks. I found the limit of the wire and moved, where I soon greeted by another wire; this time at shin level.

Searching for booby traps was my first introduction to a hidden type of fear. Years later, I would hear about shredding the bodies of my brothers in battle. But later they were called IEDs (improvised explosive devices). I would meet one first hand years later in the Kunar valley.

I continued to negotiate through the horrors of this haunted forest and there I realized something. I was alone. This was perhaps the most alone I felt during Parris Island. It was a refreshing idea at first. However, the darkness into the reality of war soon came over me. A warrior must walk into this darkness alone when it is his time. Warriors walk holding hands with death in this deadly profession.

Sweat fell upon me as I stealthily walked in the forest. Explosions and the faint yells of fallen recruits echoed and illuminated the night's sky. It was beautiful to walk there in the flower of my youth, embarking on this grand adventure. I felt my LBE hanging a bit loser that it should have on my hips, a consequence from the never-ending weight loss experienced in training. I licked the salty sweat from the top of my lips and soon felt solace as the edge of the tree line came into sight. I moved and found the edge of this haunted forest.

NIGHT ASSAULT COURSE

My Company formed up again in squads at the start point under the folds of darkness. The night's sky was illuminated by flares and the DIs instructed us to close our shooting eye when the night turned into day. There is something eerily beautiful about night flares. I find it unnerving, regardless if it is under the blanket of training or in the fiery hearth of combat.

It was thrilling to move as death under the cover of darkness. I sprinted to the first assault wall and began checking for booby traps before jumping over. A Drill Instructor from a neighboring platoon came to my side and spoke to me. His voice was not at the fearful level that is usually expected of DIs. Rather, it was mature, calm, and collected.

"Come on, move, move, move! There is no time."

I met eyes with the DI who I had seen more than once on the island. I responded and moved over the wall. I continued the assault course, jumping over walls and crawling under barbed wire. But the DI's voice just struck me. It was just so different. I heard this tone in a man's voice again. The next time was in combat.

PUGIL STICK TUNNEL

Recruits were given one last go at the pugil stick arena prior to the Crucible. Following the A-Line shooting events, the recruits howled with rage to face their final obstacle. I was fit, confident, and menacing. Best of all, I was desensitized to fear.

I heard my platoon was going to back to the arena one last time. I licked my lips for another chance to lock in combat. My body was a well-oiled machine for war. My endurance, strength, and agility were at super athletic levels. I was ready for anything.

1084 moved out and halted near a tree line near the pugil stick rings. I was a bit confused as to why we formed up here, a bit far from the rings. The CCIs strode toward us like the hunters of men they were, with their lean muscles gleaming in the sunlight. They briefed us on the upcoming event.

This event was different. Recruits would not square up in front of their opponents as they did earlier in boot camp. In the first few weeks of training I began each fight facing my opponent. I stared deeply into his eyes and took the time to read him. An experienced fighter can learn a great deal regarding the quality of the man he is about to fight just by peering into his eyes.

In those few fleeting seconds, I asked my opponent so many questions.

"Will you back down from me? Are you afraid? Are you aggressive? Will be come at me directly or are you a patient fighter? What is your name? Are you meaner than me?"

No such luxury of a stare down prior to fighting would be afforded to us this time as I would soon find out.

"Listen up, recruits. Once you are given the order to run the trail, it is game on! Do you understand that?"

"Sir, Yes Sir!" we replied.

"Run though the woods and you will come to the arena. You are clear to engage the moment you see your opponent? Do you understand that?"

"Sir, Yes Sir!"

The brief was simple enough. I was hungry for the fight. The first battle was one on one engagements. The second involved paired matches.

My platoon moved closer to the wood line and the first fighters were dressed for battle. One at a time, recruits were dressed for battle and ran off into the dark forest. Off to my right at about 50 meters I watched them, my enemy. Another Platoon from my company prepared themselves for combat. They waited at the halt, dressed only in tanned T-shirts, cammie trousers, and their Jungle boots. We would be fighting our clones, so to speak. These men were chiseled and molded out of the same fiery hearth as we were. We would soon slam bodies against the same stones we were made from. I would fight myself in the upcoming bouts.

More and more of the recruits waded into the unknown that the forest held in its dark shadows. I have always loved hiking in the woods and still do. Growing up as a hunter, the forest was my home. I can feel and sense all things in my soul when I venture in such places. Here I am the wolf and I will slaughter whatever and whoever crosses my path. Fear me.

My turn was up and I dressed for the contest. My face was blank, as I decided that there was nothing any longer to be afraid of. I merely accepted the contest at hand and swallowed my anxiety. The CCI gave me a pre-combat inspection and cleared me for battle. It was time to suit up and punch in.

I held at the ready position and gazed at the forest floor. I always enjoyed how the shadows on the forest floor danced so brilliantly for me. It is this calm that all warriors know. One can only find this type of calm prior to a cataclysmic event. I breathed in the sweet scent of the forest and smiled. I did not feel fear any more. I had become it.

These moments prior to a fight compose the final peace that perhaps may ever grace our lives. One learns to savor this short segment of time. You gulp it like a sweet breath of cool air before taking a long swim under water. You swallow it and keep it in your lungs. In battle, one must fight to have the right to merely breathe.

Warriors know the truth about life. It is not a gift that can be merely be left out in the open without a guard. Many people go on about their materialistic consumer lives without a care in the world. Many simply wander and graze upon the bitch of peace. If one were to look upon the herd of humanity, one could guess that we were, in fact, dumb animals. Have you ever gazed upon a herd of herbivores on the plains of Africa?

Herd animals live their lives grazing upon the plains. Here they mate, eat, sleep, and die. Perhaps they live carefree lives to the casual observer. However, take a moment and study them. They eat and walk to and fro. However, they take moments to pause, several times in a minute. They are not looking for food. Rather, they are looking for those that may think of them as food.

Many people live in this world, where they believe that danger is only seen on CNN or in far off countries over the horizon. These grass eaters can in fact be roused to excitement by certain traumatic events such as an attack on the homeland. For a short amount of time, these herbivores may pick their head up every once in a while and keep an eye open for potential threats. They may even tie a yellow ribbon around the tree in their front yard. However, this awareness is extremely short lived.

Warriors know better. Like wolves on patrol in the forest of the world, they constantly halt and smell the air. They smell for potential prey and for the predators that are hunting them. Warriors know that life and freedom itself must be guarded.

"Get ready, recruit!" The CCI called out to me.

My eyes open.

"Bring it, motherfucker...."

The whistle blast initiated the action. I take off sprinting, my speed slightly hindered by my protective equipment. The shadows flutter much more quickly across my eyes. The scene is too perfect for me. The temperature on the island during September was in the 70's or so. A gift as compared to the sweltering winds in the summer.

I saw a bend in the trail and I sensed the arena waiting for me in just a few feet. The bend served a purpose like everything else on this island. This change in trajectory forced recruits to slow down. My masters were all too aware of the power that was forged in our young chiseled bodies. If we were to collide at each other at a dead sprint, the chance for injury would undoubtedly be increased.

I turned as sharply as I could and immediately saw the entrance to my wood chip filled arena. I increased my pace and caught sight of my opponent as I entered.

It's only you and me, my brother. But at this moment we are not brothers attempting to attain the same title. Rather, you are him: my enemy. I will charge you and attempt to smash the life out of you.

Undoubtedly you will try to do the same to me. I don't do this because I hate you. I do this because I have been ordered to. The order means more than fear or obedience.

I follow orders because I know that is what I have to do in order to stay alive. These orders will preserve me and my comrades. These orders are the truth.

I will end you.

I catch his eyes in the tenth of a second before we collide. He has bright hazel eyes. I know his look, because it is the same look I have in my eyes. He is young, beautiful, and most of all powerful, just like me.

We connect and trade blows. The engagement is horribly violent. I can still hear our grunts as we roared at each other like lions on the African Savannah. Time slowed down in that engagement, as it does in all battles.

Perhaps warriors slow time down, as these moments may be the last segments of time in our lives. Perhaps we cherish where we breathe or have power over all our limbs.

My battles, whether they were mock bayonet fights or full on fire fights, may only last but a few seconds in time. However, each of these seconds are more influential than complete years of life. This feeling is amplified in particular when the warrior involved in this particular battle is a young man.

A whistle blasts ends this short lived but passionate contest with one another. He and I lashed at each other with every fiber of muscle in our possession. However, a mere signal from one of the DIs and we stopped dead in our tracks. The Drill Instructors seemed to have the power to halt this tremendous cascade of death and destruction in which we poured onto each other. The attack ceased and I traded one last glance into his eyes. We have nothing to say to one another. Warriors rarely do. Our eyes tell what we want and who we are.

Many warriors have trouble communicating with those who have not tasted the wine of battle. Many rather say, "They simply won't understand."

Maybe they are correct in this assumption. Can people talk to virgins about sex? (See Dave Grossman's on killing.) No. Can we talk to someone about good wine if they have never wet their lips on a nice glass of Pinot Noir? No. Perhaps the same can be said of those that have never sampled battle.

This man and I never spoke again after this passionate dance of death. I wonder about him still. He lives there now in my thoughts, like those women you may have seen as a young man, but never spoke to. Instead, he lives there as a silent actor in what has become the early screenplay to my warrior thoughts.

CRUCIBLE EVE

Nothing reinforces the fact that humans are animals like the ability to feel tension in the air the night prior to a large military operation or an intense exercise. My stomach was in knots for the long anticipated 55-hour test called "The Crucible" which awaited each of one of the recruits in platoon 1084. The next two days would encompass some of the most intense training I would ever endure in my military career.

The ALICE packs were carefully packed, checked, and re-checked for the test ahead. Lights out came and as I lay there in my rack, I thought of the exciting prospect that I was within striking distance of becoming a United States Marine. As I entered into the mystic peaceful folds of sleep as an interesting mix of excitement, nerves, and fear was carried by my veins into the furthest reaches of my body and into the depths of my soul. Sleep found me and I dosed off.

MORNING

At around 0300, the lights came on and for the first time on Parris Island there was no screaming or yelling. There simply was no need. The fear within the recruit's souls was enough to motivate everyone to speedily gear up as if a Chinese infantry brigade was marching on Washington D.C. The Drill Instructors were no longer wearing their distinctive "Smoky Bear covers." Rather, they were adorned in the same soft covers the recruits wore.

SIX MILE FORCED MARCH.

C company assembled outside like it did dozens of times before. My pack felt good on my shoulders and my rifle rested upon my right shoulder at sling arms. The cool September blew a pleasant and familiar breeze upon my skin. This was it. I was starting my last and final test that separated me from that coveted Eagle Globe and Anchor. I sighed the sweet air into my lungs and waited for the command.

It came: "FOOOORWARD MAAAAARCH!"

This was one command that will forever live within the record of my warrior soul. C company stepped off at a good pace and moved toward the woodlands surrounding the air field on Parris Island. My blood was ignited with excitement only felt on occasions such as Christmas morning. The pace was kept smart and we made the long hike from garrison out to the training area. It was hard to even imagine that I was this close to becoming a United States Marine. My heart glowed with anticipation.

A grey dawn and light drizzle greeted the recruits as night slowly turned to day. My platoon arrived at the assembly area as the new day came to be. The recruits were separated into squads and we covered our ALICE packs with ponchos. None of the recruits knew what to expect next and each man prepared themselves for whatever horrible challenges that lay just beyond the next clump of trees. My squad soon received orders to stack arms. My squad neatly and carefully stacked our rifles and moved out.

A Close Combat Instructor waited for us with his pugil stick equipment. I smiled at this first event and awaited my turn for a fight. I geared up and walked into the ring. The Instructor asked my opponent and me if we held any special position in the platoon. The recruit indicated that he as the Protestant lay reader.

The DI asked me and I answered that I was in fact the Catholic lay reader. The ironies of the situation made us all laugh, prior to locking sticks.

My squad did well in the battle but the glory was short lived as we moved to the next series of warrior stations. The recruits spent the remainder of the day conducting numerous problem solving stations that included moving casualties over casualty courses, forced marches, and other assault courses. A different recruit was put in charge each time we moved to a new scenario. The tempo continued to be long and hard as each man attempted to ration the 2.5 MREs issued out. We were not told when to eat. Rather rationing was placed on ourselves.

My body continued to grow tired and day soon turned into night. My platoon was ordered to conduct a five-mile resupply hike, in which we were burdened with additional ammunition boxes, water, and supplies. We shared the burden of the extra weight, each man according to his ability. Few things teach a warrior about how strong they in fact are like carrying supplies through a grueling ruck march. I panted heavily on the pace, keeping my eyes transfixed on the man ahead of me. We were moving at a fast pace, almost five miles per hour. I prayed for the hike to be over at first. Then eventually, like all the other pain on the island, I accepted the pain. I became the pain.

The hike came to an end and finally we arrived back at the rest area. I dumped my back and bedded down for a brief four-hour sleep.

DAY 2

Morning was greeted by yet another foot march. By the end of this 54- hour test, 1084 completed nearly 55 miles on foot. My body continually ached under the burden of my pack and equipment; yet I moved on. More warrior leader problem stations greeted us and became continually more challenging as our bodies and minds fatigued under the stresses of this final test.

1084 picked up and moved to another assembly area near a rifle range as was foretold by the shooting that echoed in the air. My squad was issued ammunition and dropped packs. My squad followed the Instructor to an assembly point within the wood line and were placed in a file. Live ammo was issued to us. I was locked and loaded a magazine.

Slamming a live round into your chamber changes the world for a warrior. The rifle becomes alive with this bullet inside it, waiting to bring death to the world. It is like giving a soul to a body. You become more than a man at that moment as you have the power to destroy life. This feeling would come to me again during my patrols in combat later in life in the horrid valleys of the Pech River Valley, Afghanistan.

A Warrior crosses a line when he locks and loads his weapon. In doing this act you become that Grim Reaper, and the stuff of nightmares. You have the power to turn your enemy's body into that coveted pink mist. In an instant, you have the ability to expel breath from lungs and a soul from a body.

I was ready to become death.

Although it was September, it was still brutally hot. Sweat trickled across my body from my face to my hands. We walked in single file toward the release point. Our rifles were staggered, facing opposite directions, as we walked — a technique derived from the echoes of Vietnam. We waited for the green smoke before charging to our shooting positions.

The smoke emitted from a smoke grenade and it provided concealment as well as served as the signal. My squad charged through the smoke that instantly blanketed the terrain before us. It was an intense moment in time, as it was the first time in my life that I ran with my weapon locked and loaded. As I approached my firing position, my fellow recruits around me screamed with primordial yells that were forged in us during our time on the island. I jumped down into a bunker. After clearing sweat from my brow, I took aim at the silhouettes and sent steel down range. I wondered if battle would be like this, sending steel under a haze of confusion and heat. I would wait many years before I would find out.

EVE OF FINAL MARCH.

1084 returned to the B huts following the day on the plains of Mars. There was a not foot without blisters amongst the ranks. Navy Corpsmen perused the ranks, checking for any bad injuries that a recruit might be hiding. It did not matter how hurt we all were. All that separated us from glory was a mere nine-mile hump. The feeling of anticipation and excitement was contagious. We all were ready for the promise and the end of this horrible place.

I dozed off under the beautiful thoughts of embracing my girlfriend while wearing a Marine uniform. I closed my eyes and fell deep into a peaceful slumber.

9 MILES TO GLORY.

I awoke to my final morning of not being a United States Marine. I hastily packed my rucksack and ensured I knotted and double knotted my boots. My hands still tingle with excitement now even as I write. There were coolers of water and punch for us to consume prior to stepping off. I was ready.

1084 assembled outside and the beautiful formation of recruits glimmered in the moonlight. The chaplains circulated in the ranks and were easy to see by their glowing crucifixes made out of chem lights. The command "forward march" was given and we moved out toward promised destinies.

This time, the "little end" was placed at the front of the formation, keeping the pace smart. We moved. The excitement of the glory that waited at the end of the march kept fatigue to a minimum. Rosy fingered dawn soon approached and beautiful light cascaded down from the heavens. The Drill Instructors began leading us in marching cadences, singing beautiful songs such as "*In her hair she wore a yellow ribbon. She's waiting for that young Marine... so far, far, away...*"

Visions of seeing my family and my girl warmed my blood and dulled the pain of my mangled feet. We approached the main side of Parris Island and the buildings came into view. "Holy fuck." I thought as we neared garrison. I could not believe that I was actually going to become a United States Marine.

EAGLE, GLOBE, AND ANCHOR

All pain left my body as the parade deck came into view. The early morning light cascaded unto the land and set the scene. We stepped on the parade deck and were placed back into quickstep and finally ordered to halt. We dropped our packs and stacked arms.

This was it.

We moved to the Iwo Jima Memorial flanked by bleachers seated by hundreds of Marine veterans of all different ages. Here, hundreds of recruits who were barely able to walk, hobbled in this area and somehow managed to dress themselves neatly into ranks for the formation.

Pure sanctity electrified the silent air. The wind danced and birds chirped. The air felt the same way it did before a large battle. We waited…

"Company, Attention. Present… Arms!"

We snapped in unison and awaited the colors to be raised. The national anthem followed. Chills flowed down my spine then, as it does every single time it plays. Tears streamed down my eyes and cleaned the dirt out of my sight.

"Order arms!"

The Drill Instructors moved, holding the coveted symbol of the Eagle, Globe and Anchor in their hands. Warriors cry because there is simply no other way to express the emotions felt. In the entire formation and in the audience, a dry eye was hard to find. I heard the sniffling by all the heroes around me. I could not stop the tears from falling. This was one of the most joyous moments of my entire life.

The scene was too perfect to conceive. A gentle breeze graced our tired and sweaty bodies. The crisp flag silently barked in the early fall southern air. The song "I am proud to an American" played softly in the air. To this day, the tune still brings tears of joy to my eyes.

The sad thing about this moment in life, as with all great moments in one's life, is that they only exist in a few heartbeats. You only get to experience this temporary moment in life but once in a lifetime. Like a beautiful butterfly, the delicate wings in this wonderful flight can only exist in mere seconds.

We arrive at the island and crawl on the ground like grubby little caterpillars. We crawl upon the Earth like disgusting undisciplined creatures that know nothing regarding the art of war. During the crucible, we spin a cocoon to undergo the metamorphosis into these machines of war and destruction.

We emerge as dark, beautiful Grim Reapers of War.

The Drill Instructors were now at my squad and were making their way down toward me. I dared not move a muscle; not now in this most sanctified of moments. However, the Marine veterans were clearly visible in my line of sight. The pure emotion of this moment could be seen in each of their eyes as well. It seemed that no one ever forgets the pain involved in one's journey in becoming a United States Marine.

We carry this pain felt on the fields on Parris Island or MCRD San Diego for the length of our entire lives. It is this pain that creates that adrenaline-laced violence that all Marines seem to be able to recall with a push of a button. We carry these scars with us for all the days of our lives. This pain lives in our wrinkles and in our arteries. Once we taste these hard lessons, we never forget them.

Finally, my time had come. SSgt Staley looked into my eyes, placed the Eagle, Globe, and Anchor into my hands and said, "Welcome to the family." I replied with, "Thank you, sir." A feeling of undesirable bliss entered my blood and jolted me with limitless pride. I had become a Marine. The hours of pain and discipline had finally paid off in this victory of victories.

I was a United States Marine.

WARRIOR BREAKFAST

The ceremony was complete and some of the instant euphoria began to wear off. What followed was not true glory, rather it was the very thing that I kept hidden for the past 24 hours or so. It was pain. We all felt it.

We all began to hobble back to our ALICE packs. It is always after climbing the mountain where the true measure of pain sets in. My feet were a hot mess of hot spots and puss filled blisters. Every step was excruciating. However, the conditioning at boot camp gave me the proper skill set to deal with this pain. Many lay people think that intense military training teaches one to ignore pain. Nothing can be further from the truth. Rather, the truth is that military training teaches one to accept the pain. Like fucked up warrior Buddhists monks, we accept this factor of face wincing pain and merely allow it to become a part of us.

I bit my lip as we made our slow march back to the barracks. Another feeling was beginning to make its way into my psyche and the other warriors around me: hunger. In the past 55 hours, we had subsisted off a mere 2.5 MREs. We were ready for the prize of the warrior breakfast that awaited us.

The barracks looked like a five-star hotel to my tired body. We set our ALICE packs near our racks and secured our rifles. We moved to the chow hall. This was the first meal in nearly three months where we could relax and chat to each other calmly as comrades.

The meal tasted like fine cuisine. I felt relieved to finally rest on a comfortable chair with all the food I could eat. I made it. My God… I became a Marine. I cannot begin to explain the amount of pride one feels from finishing this road. To date, it is still amongst my proudest accomplishments of my life.

In time, my stomach was full. We were not told when to walk back to the barracks or when to finish the meal. Instead, we were instructed to eat all that we wanted and to return to the barracks when we were ready. It was time for me to take my leave. I hobbled back to the barracks on the minced pieces of foot meat that all professional warriors who have carried a pack and a rifle can tell you about over a beer. I hobbled back as a Marine.

FINAL DAYS

My last week on the island consisted of administrative matters and graduation rehearsal. The final Sunday on the island, we were granted a few hours for recruit liberty. We dressed in our Charlie's and were allowed to visit the PX, make phone calls, and just be on our own.

I marched straight to the calling center. I called my parents for a few minutes and talked about seeing them that coming Thursday for graduation. Next I called my girl.

Women for all warriors seem to hold the keys to hopes, dreams, and pain. Love kept me going, as it would later in my warrior career. Love alone gives warriors the ability to continue the horrible journeys to the darkest corners of the Earth. Love becomes Hope.

I dialed her phone number and prayed that she would answer the phone. I was in luck.

"Hello," she said.

238 | ANTONIO M. SALINAS

"Hi, Lindsay. I love you. I'm a Marine." I said.

We talked for a good while exchanging proclamations of love and desire in the manner that you only declare with your first love. Linda wrote to me nearly every day. Her daily letters lifted my heart in a way that I can never thank her enough for. Love truly gives breath to a warrior.

GRADUATION

"Once a Marine, always a Marine." To those who have not earned the title, this line may appear to be cliché'. However, this statement will always ring true in my mind and soul. Marines all share the same time developing in the womb of chaos. Like babies hearing their mother's voices in the womb, Marines share the same experience. Marines of all ages, even separated by generations, have the same mother. This lady molds us into the warriors that we become. She grooms our minds, bodies, and souls for the prom date called War. When Marines graduate, they wear their dress uniforms to prom. They march confidently into the fires of chaos without hesitation. Marines march triumphantly into this fog of war.

All the rehearsals and inspections were over. We packed our uniforms neatly that night. I was overly excited to see my family and girlfriend.

Morning came and we dressed for the last time in the squad bay of Platoon 1084. I will forever miss that place of pain and what made me into what I am today. I dressed in the fashion of the Marines, My shirt, shirt stays on my socks, then my trousers. We were ready.

To this day, piecing the individual memories of the graduation ceremony is truly a blur. Nearly nineteen years later, I can barely remember marching out to graduation. Perhaps, because that ceremony was more of a formality. There was one thing absent from that moment of time on the island. There was no chaos.

Following the parade we waited for the words that would dismiss us from the island and release us into the world of the Marines…

"Platoon 1084; dismissed."

"Aye, Aye Sir. Ooh Rah!"

With an about face I ran to embrace my loved ones.

My journey to becoming a Marine was over. My voyage toward war was just beginning.

Me on graduation day October 9, 1998

My return to the island in 2007

CONCLUSION: ONCE A MARINE, ALWAYS A MARINE

The path of becoming a United States Marine is one caught in the lore of American Military history, Hollywood, and in the eyes of all who are called Marine. It is the path for warriors. On Parris Island, a man drinks of what I call "Marine Corps magic." A Marine never forgets their time spent suffering on these parade fields, woodlands, rifle ranges, and sand. The lessons, whether learned at Parris Island or MCRD San Diego, are never forgotten.

For many, being a Marine will be one of the greatest things that they attempt in their lives. Many of us, including me, get a tattoo as a memento to remember their time.

Marines have always performed exceptionally well in the chaotic fires of combat. Perhaps this is because they are made in this never-ending maelstrom of chaos, pain, and fear. Eventually, we become these things that we feared so much.

You can see proof of this grand statement by looking into the eyes of anyone who has earned the title Marine. Whatever becomes of them or the path they lead in their life, they will always carry the pride of the Marines deeply rooted within them. There are some lessons one never forgets.

MARINES ARE JUST DIFFERENT

There is just something different about Marines. If you have ever met one or even loved one, you know this is true. They are warriors who seek the ideal of warrior virtue. We are these strange, over zealous, and over confident stoic warriors. Many Marines have been born in the wrong time, and would have thrived in the hoplite armies of ancient Greece. But what is it that makes Marines unique as a class of warriors?

Following graduation, I traveled home to Michigan with my family. I was different, like we all were. For years, I wondered what was it in this concoction of Parris Island magic that made Marines so different from other services. Sure, Marines bitch about long hours and going to the field just like every other Solider, Sailor or Airman does. However, there is just something different about us.

THE TRUTH OF COMBAT: BATTLEFIELDS OF AFGHANISTAN

I finished my enlistment in 2002, without going to war. I was briefly mobilized in 2003 for the Iraq campaign. However, this war eluded me again. Following graduate school, I took a commission in the Army as an Infantry officer. I finally learned what makes Marines so different from every other branch of service, not at college or at Infantry Officer Basic course. Rather, I learned in those horrible dark valleys of Kunar Province, Afghanistan.

Kunar was my school of combat and where I tasted that strong wine known as war. Once a warrior tastes war, they are changed forever. When I came home from war, I began to write on the experience of war. Then it hit me.

I figured out why Marines are so different.

THE ANSWER

The answer came clear to me after my first firefight over a decade after boot camp. There was something oddly familiar about the sensations that I felt in combat. Upon reflection, I realized that I felt some of them before while at Parris Island.

In military training, the goal is to attempt to simulate battlefield conditions through sleep deprivation, stress, hunger, and exhaustion. However, it is extremely difficult to replicate that innate feeling of fear that you may actually die. Self-preservation becomes a factor during the heat of battle.

The levels of stress, fear, and intensity I felt in combat was honestly somewhat similar to the levels I experienced as an 18-year-old while at Parris Island. While of course I did not fear for my life in boot camp, the Marines have at least come close to synthesizing to some degree the fear, intensity, and stress one may experience in combat. I was injected with this synthetic battlefield serum at Parris Island. It is this shared baptism of violence that makes one of the basic tenets of the Marine Corps warrior culture.

I was heard a Marine state: "I have been in combat… but I have never been as afraid as I was at Parris Island."

When I first heard this quote, I though it was complete bullshit. I don't think that I was more afraid on Parris Island. However, the intensity is nearly there.

On a 0-10 point scale measuring fear and stress, combat tops the scale. I have never made it past a 7 in the majority of my military training. However, the fear and stress I felt at Parris Island compares to the stress felt in battle at about 9-9.5 scale. The even more amazing thing is that Marine Drill Instructors maintain that level of intensity on the recruits for three months. This is the very basis of what I call Marine Corps magic.

All Marines graduate Parris Island with a synthetic 1,000-yard stare. It is this experience which seems to separate them from other branches and instills a great deal of pride within its members and lasts a lifetime.

To this day, it is one of the epic experiences of my life. After Parris Island, a Marine will go on to do many different things. Some may go on to serve for decades and participate in a collage of engagements. Others may only serve for a few years and never hear the mind sickening whip-snap of an incoming bullet. Regardless of the path they take, he or she will never forget those three months they spent either at Parris Island or MCRD San Diego.

I can never thank the Marine Corps enough for its positive impact on my life. Perhaps you are next.

Truly, once you become a Marine, you are always a Marine.
Semper Fi. July 20th, 2017

ABOUT THE AUTHOR

Antonio Salinas was born and raised in Allen Park, Michigan. His youth was spent dabbling in combative sports and hunting in the woodlands of Michigan. Upon graduating from Allen Park High School in 1998, Antonio enlisted in the United States Marine Corps where he served as a geospatial intelligence  analyst, then a martial arts instructor trainer, and later an intelligence chief. Following his time in the Marines, Antonio attended Eastern Michigan University and gained his Bachelors in History and Political Science. Antonio then pursued graduate school where he enrolled in Army ROTC and attained his Masters in History. Antonio was commissioned as a 2nd Lieutenant in 2007 and has served in both Afghanistan and Iraq. Antonio continues to serve in uniform as a history instructor at West Point, NY.

CPSIA information can be obtained
at www.ICGtesting.com
Printed in the USA
BVOW09s0727220418
514082BV00019B/1105/P